12 14

SWEDEN

COPENHAGEN
Roskilde
Korsör Köge
Naestved
Rödvig
Lund
Malmö
Ystad
Trälleborg

BALTIC

Simrishamn
Sandhammaren

Bornholm
(to Denmark)
Rönne

SEA

J. Lebskie

Falster
Nyköbing
Moen

Rügen
Sassnitz
Zingst
Barth

Pomeranian Bay

Darwolo

Fehmarn
Warnemünde
Warburg
adt
K.B.
Bad Doberan
Wismar

Stralsund
Greifswald
Rostock
Demmin
Güstrow

Peene
Wolgast
Anklam

Usedom I. Kolobrzeg
Swinoujcie
Wolin I.
Szczecinek

Koszalin

Kamien Pomorski
Gryfice
Resko

Szczecinek
Czaplinek
Wierz-
chowo
Zlotow

54

Bialogard
Bobolice

MECKLENBURG-VORPOMMERN
verin
Plau
Parchim
Krakow
See
Müritz

Stettiner
Haff
Neu
brandenburg
Neustrelitz
Brüssow
Passewalk

Szczecin
Stargard

Walcz
Choszczno
Czlopa

Pila

Wittstock
Wittenberge
Kyritz
Dömitz
Neuruppin
Eberswalde
Trenzlau
Schwedt
Pyrzyce
Chojna
Gartz
Gorzow Wlkp.
Mysliborz
Notec

Kyzyz
Czarnkow
Wagrowice

BRANDENBURG
Rathenow
Spandau
BERLIN

Kosizyn
Szamotuly
Miedzychod

Poznan

Burg
Schönebeck
Belzig
Brandenburg
Baruth
Luckenwalde

Frankf
Oder
Mledzyrzecz

POLAND

Grodzisk
Kościan

52

Dessau
Wittenberg
Lübben
Gubin
Zielona Gora
Leszno

ANHALT
Aschersleben
Köthen
Bitterfeld
Luckau
Jüterbog
Spremberg

Forst
Nowa
Sol
Wschawa

Rowicz

Halle
Merseburg
Weissenfels
Naumburg
Zeitz

Torgau
Wurzen
Mühlberg
Riesa
Meissen

SAXONY
Senftenberg
Crossen
Bautzen
Görlitz
Warnsd
Zittau

Zary
Sprotawa
Zagan
Glogow

Boleslawiec
Chojnow

Lubin
Trzebnica

Legnica
Jelenia
Gora
Wroclaw

Swidnica

ANGIAZ
Gera
Zwickau
Greiz
Chemnitz
Annaberg
Teplice
Pirna
Freiberg
Decin
Liberec
Jablonec
Gordo
Walbrzych

Boguszów
Nowy
Rudu

Plauen
Chomutov
Usti (Aussig)
Litomerice
Mlada Boleslav
Trautenau Mts.
Nachod
Klodzko

ast 12 14 16

COLLINS'
PHRASE BOOKS

COLLINS'
PHRASE BOOKS
FRENCH: GERMAN: ITALIAN: SPANISH: RUSSIAN: PORTUGUESE: SCANDINAVIAN

INSTANTANEOUS IN USE

The complete Index, practical subdivision of Subjects, and clear bold type, ensure that the required phrases are found immediately.

EASILY UNDERSTOOD

The clear and accurate pronunciation of every word may be read simply as English syllables, and the use of confusing symbols is avoided.

UP-TO-DATE

The most modern requirements of travellers on the Continent are fully dealt with, including Air Travel, Motoring, etc.

ACCURATE

The sentences are expressed in the latest idioms by experts in both languages, while the information included has been officially checked.

PRACTICAL

The practical choice of sentences, the introductory advice and the many hints on difficulties are invaluable to tourists and business men alike.

COLLINS'
PHRASE BOOKS

GERMAN

Edited by
ZOË L. RUSSELL, M.A.

COLLINS
LONDON AND GLASGOW

GENERAL EDITOR: G. F. MAINE

First Published 1951
Latest Reprint 1961

Printed in Great Britain
COLLINS CLEAR-TYPE PRESS

CONTENTS

	Page
INTRODUCTION	9
General—Central European Time—Trains—Local Information—Meals—Tipping—Amusements—German-speaking Switzerland	
NOTE ON PRONUNCIATION SCHEME	11
CONVERSION TABLES	14
PHRASES IN COMMON USE	17
Writing Letters	24
Telephoning	25
TRAVELLING BY TRAIN	26
Arriving	26
Changing	27
Departing	28
At the Station—Luggage—Left-luggage—General	32
Time-tables	38
On the Train	39
TRAVELLING BY BOAT	43
TRAVELLING BY AIR	46
CUSTOMS	49
ACCOMMODATION	52
Engaging Rooms	53
In the Hotel	55
Hotel Office	58
Leaving the Hotel	59
LAUNDRY	62
LOCAL TRAVELLING—EXCURSIONS	63
Finding the Way	63
Going by Train	65
Going by Motor	66
Sight-seeing	67

CONTENTS

VISITING FRIENDS ... 73

SHOPPING ... 76
    The Tobacconist ... 76
    The Post Office ... 78
    The Chemist ... 80
    The Hairdresser ... 84
    Photography ... 86
    Bookshop and Stationer ... 87
    The Bank ... 89
    General Shopping Vocabulary ... 90
    Repairs ... 98
    The Police ... 99

ACCIDENT AND ILLNESS ... 100
    At the Dentist's ... 103

AT TABLE ... 105
    Menu and Utensils ... 108

ENTERTAINMENT ... 116
    Radio ... 120

SPORT ... 121

MOTORING ... 125

COUNTRIES AND NATIONALITIES ... 130

NUMERALS ... 134
    Weights and Measures ... 136
    Days of the Week ... 136
    Months ... 137
    Time—General Phrases ... 137
    Time—The Clock ... 138

GERMAN-ENGLISH SECTION ... 139
    Public Notices and Phrases in Common Use ... 139
    Common German Abbreviations ... 144

INDEX (German) ... 146

INDEX (English) ... 152

INHALTSVERZEICHNIS

EINFÜHRUNG
  Allgemeines—Mitteleuropäische Zeit—Züge—
  Auskunft—Mahlzeit—Trinkgeld—Vergnügungen
  —Die deutsche Schweiz

ERKLÄRUNG DER AUSSPRACHE   11

UMSETZUNG   14

ALLGEMEINE REDEWENDUNGEN   17
  Briefe schreiben   24
  Am Telephon   25

REISEN : MIT DER EISENBAHN   26
  Ankunft   26
  Umsteigen   27
  Abfahrt   28
  Auf dem Bahnhof—Gepäck—Handgepäck—All-
    gemeines   32
  Fahrpläne   38
  Im Zuge   39

SEEFAHRT   43

LUFTFAHRT   46

ZOLL   49

HOTELS UND PENSIONEN   52
  Zimmer mieten   53
  Im Hotel   55
  Am Büro   58
  Abreisen   59

WÄSCHE   63

INLANDSREISEN, AUSFLÜGE
  Nach dem Wege fragen   63
  Die Bahnfahrt   65

INLANDSREISEN, AUSFLÜGE—*Continued*
Die Autofahrt 66
Sehenswürdigkeiten 67

BESUCHE MACHEN 73

EINKÄUFE 76
Das Zigarrengeschäft 76
Das Postamt 78
Die Apotheke 80
Der Friseur 84
Das Photogeschäft 86
Buch- und Papierhandlung 87
Die Bank 89
Wortliste zum Einkaufen 90
Reparaturen 96
Die Polizei 99

UNFALL UND KRANKHEIT 100
Beim Zahnarzt 103

ZU TISCH 105
Speisen und Tafelgerät 108

VERGNÜGUNGEN 116
Radio 120

SPORT 121

AUTOFAHREN 125

LÄNDER UND VÖLKER 130

ZAHLWÖRTER 134
Masse und Gewichte 136
Tage der Woche 136
Monate 137
Zeit—häufige Ausdrücke 137
Zeit—die Uhr 138

DEUTSCH-ENGLISCH 139
Gebräuchliche Phrasen 139
Abkürzungen 144

WORTVERZEICHNIS (Deutsch) 146

WORTVERZEICHNIS (Englisch) 152

INTRODUCTION

THIS little book is more than a collection of useful phrases. It also answers many of the questions which a traveller in the German-speaking countries will wish to ask about food, travel, customs, and so on.

Of course, it is not possible to give precise details about all those things, because time-tables, rates of exchange, passport and customs regulations change. Up-to-date information may be obtained from travel agencies. Labour exchanges also supply information about passports, and banks about currency rates and regulations. A table is provided on page 13 in which the current rate of exchange should be entered.

Travel in West Germany is unrestricted, but it is more difficult to go to West Berlin, and an agent should be consulted. It is usually possible to visit East Berlin and East Germany, but the regulations are strict and it is essential to consult an agent or a British consul in Germany. A visa is required for the Eastern sector.

CENTRAL EUROPEAN TIME.—German (and Swiss) time is one hour ahead of Greenwich Mean Time, i.e., noon in Britain is 1 p.m. in Germany. During British Summer Time the hours are equal, as in Germany the clock is not put forward.

TRAINS.—There are two main types of train in Germany: the slow train, or Personenzug, and the express or Schnellzug. (See "Travelling by Train.") For travel by express train a small supplementary charge (Zuschlag) is made. This does not apply in Switzerland. Visitors to Switzerland may find it worth while to take advantage of the reduced rates for rail travel offered under the Holiday Ticket system. Details may be obtained from the office of the Swiss Federal Railways in London.

In Germany seat reservations (Platzkarten) may be had at a cost of about 1 D Mark. Sleeping car accommodation, where available, is good and cheaper than in Britain. Second-class travel is usually comfortable, but some slow trains have wooden seats. Restaurant cars serve meals and refreshments at almost any time. In Germany the distinction between smoking and non-smoking compartments is strictly observed.

LOCAL INFORMATION.—This may be obtained in any city from offices marked *Auskunft*.

MEALS.—In Germany and Switzerland breakfast consists of coffee and rolls, but a more substantial meal may usually be had on request. Lunch and dinner are the main meals. Afternoon tea is not provided in hotels unless specially ordered, and very few people understand the art of tea-making. Coffee is usually very good, but pure coffee is not cheap owing to the high price of beans in Germany.

The café is very popular in Germany, and provides a convenient meeting-place for friends or for the discussion of business. Newspapers and magazines are often provided, and one is not obliged to leave as soon as one has consumed one's refreshment. In the small restaurants known as *Tanz-bars* one can dine and dance fairly cheaply. Dinner dances are also popular in the large hotels.

TIPPING.—This is a vexed question when service charge is added to the bill, as it often is ; waiters expect, or at least hope for, additional recognition of their services. Where no service charge is made, the usual amount is ten per cent of the bill. Taxi-drivers do not expect a large tip and will be quite happy with a very small sum.

AMUSEMENTS.—Light music, in the form of *Operette*, is particularly good, and does not depend on a knowledge of German. Intimate review is often excellent, but demands a knowledge of German and of topical and local affairs. Music-hall (*Variété*) is good and easier to appreciate.

GERMAN-SPEAKING SWITZERLAND lies in the north and north-east of the country, the part nearest Germany. It includes the frontier town of Basle (Basel), Zürich and Berne (Bern), the federal capital. Roughly three-quarters of the population of Switzerland speak German, but in the cities and resorts many people also speak English and French. The German spoken in Switzerland sounds very different from that of Germany, but in talking to foreign visitors the Swiss will adapt his pronunciation accordingly. The chief differences in pronunciation between Swiss German and standard German are in the vowel sounds :

German *au* (ow) is pronounced (oo) in Swiss German; thus German *aus* (owce) sounds like (oos).

German *ei* (ī) is pronounced (ee), so that *Eis* (ice) sounds like (ees).

These two changes unite to baffle the stranger in the commonly used expression *aussteigen*, " to get out, alight." The standard pronunciation in Germany is (owce'-shtī-gen), but in Switzerland it is (oos'-shtee-gen). A Swiss conductor telling you to " get out here " will sound something like (here oos'-shtee-ge), the final *n* often not being sounded.

Many Swiss German words are borrowed from French. It is, for example, usual to say " mɛrci " (mair-see) instead of the German " danke " for " thank you," and the ticket collector will ask for " alle *Billets* bitte " (ull'-er bee'yay bitt'er), " all tickets please," where his German counterpart will say " alle *Fahrkarten* bitte."

NOTE ON PRONUNCIATION SCHEME

THE pronunciation of German, like that of our own language, varies widely in different parts of the country. This book is based on the standard pronunciation as used on the stage, and it will be generally understood.

The pronunciations given should be read simply as English words and phrases, with the stress placed on the syllable immediately preceding the accent mark ('). Since in some cases the pronunciation of a group of letters may differ in English according to the word in which it occurs, and since one or two German sounds cannot be accurately represented in English, the following simple rules should be remembered :

a—The German short " a " is represented by *u*, pronounced as in *trunk* (the open sound used in the South of England). It is pronounced roughly like the " a " in North of England dialects.

i, o—In general the correct value is given to the vowels " i " and " o " if the pronunciations are read as English words. In cases of doubt a stroke is placed over the letter : *ī, ō*, to denote the long sound as in *write, note*.

A mute " e " is often added to a syllable to give the correct pronunciation, and should be pronounced as in English.

For example : Streit = shtrite (as in English *kite*).
            der   =   dare (as in English).

ow is always to be pronounced as in *cow* and not as in *show*.

ü—This sound is the English " ee " made with the lips forward and rounded (in a whistling position).

ŏŏ represents a shortened form of the English *oo* as in *foot*. Thus the German pronunciation of the " u " in *unter* (ŏŏn'-ter) is similar to that of the North of England *under*.

The unmarked *oo* is pronounced as in English *boot*.

er, ur—The italic *r* should not be pronounced ; it is added to give the correct quality of the vowel preceding it.

Thus German *e* at the end of a word, represented by
" er," is to be pronounced as a separate syllable with a
sound as in English *latter*.

" ur " is the German *ö* sound. For example, *schön*
(shurn), rather like the English *urn*.

r—It is important to note that the German *r* should be
trilled (as in Scots). Thus, " warm " (varm) should
be pronounced " varrrm."

ch is pronounced as the English " sh," but with the
lips drawn back.

CH represents the guttural sound as in Scots *loch*, and
is always used after the vowels *a*, *o*, *u*.

g is always hard, as in English *get*.

y is to be sounded as in English *yes*.

oñ is used in words pronounced as with the French
nasal.

CURRENCY

The traveller should insert the prevailing rates of exchange.

WEST GERMANY

*The basic unit of West German currency is the mark, which is
divided into* 100 *pfennigs.*

10 pfennigs	=		20 marks	=
50 ,,	=		50 ,,	=
1 mark	=		100 ,,	=
5 marks	=		500 ,,	=

SWITZERLAND

*The basic unit of Swiss currency is the franc, which is divided
into* 100 *centimes.*

10 centimes	=		20 francs	=
50 ,,	=		50 ,,	=
1 franc	=		100 ,,	=
5 francs	=		500 ,,	=

CONVERSION TABLES

DISTANCE

Kilometres	*Miles*
1	⅝
2	1¼
3	1⅞
4	2½
5	3⅛
6	3¾
7	4⅜
8	5
9	5⅝
10	6¼
15	9⅜
20	12⅜
30	18⅝
40	24⅞
50	31⅛
60	37¼
70	43½
80	49¾
90	55⅞
100	62⅛
150	93¼
200	124¼
250	155⅜
300	186⅜
350	217½
400	248½
450	279⅝
500	310¾
600	372⅞
700	435
800	497⅛
900	559¼
1,000	621⅜

LENGTH and HEIGHT

Centimetres	*Inches*
1	0·39
2·54	1
10	3·94
15·2	6
25	9·85
50	19·69
100 (1 metre)	39·37

Metres	*Yards*	*Feet*
1	1·09	3′ 3·3″
2	2·19	6′ 6·7″
3	3·28	9′ 10″
4	4·37	13′ 1·4″
5	5·47	16′ 4·8″
6	6·56	19′ 8·25″
7	7·65	22′ 11·7″
8	8·74	26′ 3″
9	9·84	29′ 6·3″
10	10·94	32′ 9·67″
20	21·87	65′ 7″
30	32·80	98′ 4″
40	43·74	131′ 2″
50	54·68	164′
60	65·62	196′ 10″
70	76·55	229′ 8″
80	87·49	262′ 5″
100	109·36	328′
200	218·72	656′
400	437·44	1,312′
500	546·8	1,640′
1,000	1,093·6	3,280′
1,500	1,640·4	4,921′
5,000	3 m. 188 yds.	16,404′
10,000	6 m. 376 yds.	32.808′

WEIGHT		TEMPERATURE	
Grammes	*Ozs.*	*Centigrade*	*Fahrenheit*
100	3·53 ozs.	—18	—0·4
250	8·82 ozs.	—10	+14
454	1 lb. 0·0 ozs.	—5	23
500	1 lb. 1·6 ozs.	Zero	32
750	1 lb. 10·4 ozs.	1	33·8
		2	35·6
Kilograms	*Lbs.*	3	37·4
1	2·20	4	39·2
2	4·41	5	41
3	6·61	6	42·8
4	8·82	7	44·6
5	11·02	8	46·4
6	13·23	9	48·2
7	15·43	10	50
8	17·64	11	51·8
9	19·84	12	53·6
15	33·07	13	55·4
25	55·12	14	57·2
35	77·16	15	59·0
45	99·21	16	60·8
55	121·25	17	62·6
65	143·3	18	64·4
75	165·35	19	66·2
		20	68
Tonnes	*Tons**	25	77
1	0·98	30	86
2	1·97	40	104
3	2·95	50	122
5	4·92	60	140
7	6·89	70	158
15	14·76	80	176
25	24·6	90	194
45	44·29	100	212

* These are British Imperial tons of 2,240 lbs.

N.B. For liquid measure, area, and pressure, *see* p. 136.

CLOTHING SIZES

DRESSES AND SUITS (Women)

British	36	38	40	42	44	46
American	34	36	38	40	42	44
Continental	42	44	46	48	50	52

DRESSES AND SUITS (Junior Miss)

British	32	33	35	36	38	39
American	10	12	14	16	18	20
Continental	38	40	42	44	46	48

MEN'S SUITS AND OVERCOATS

British and American	36	38	40	42	44	46
Continental	46	48	50	52	54	56

SHIRTS

British and American	14	14½	15	15½	16	16½	17
Continental	36	37	38	39	41	42	43

SOCKS

British and American	9½	10	10½	11	11½
Continental	38-39	39-40	40-41	41-42	42-43

HATS

British and American	6½	6⅝	6¾	6⅞	7	7⅛	7¼	7⅜	7½
Continental	53	54	55	56	57	58	59	60	61

SHOES

British and American	3	4	5	6	7	8	9	10
Continental	36	37	38	39	41	42	43	44

STOCKINGS

British and American	8	8½	9	9½	10	10½
Continental	0	1	2	3	4	5

GLOVE sizes are the same in every country.

PHRASES IN COMMON USE

When addressing strange people to ask the way, etc., one should begin " Verzeihen Sie " (fair-tsi'-en zee) ; a lady is addressed politely as " Gnädige Frau " (g-nay'-dig-er frow), where " Madam " would be used in English. If she is unmarried the correct address is " Gnädiges Fräulein " (g-nay'-dig-ez froy'-line). Shop assistants, telephone operators, waitresses, etc., are addressed as " Fräulein " (froy'-line). " Herr " (hair) and " Frau " (frow) are used only in connection with the name, like " Mr." or " Mrs."

Note.—When declining an offer, Germans do not say " No, thank you," but simply " Danke " (dunk'-er) ; if one wishes to accept, say, a second helping at table, one should say " Bitte " (bitt'-er).

Yes, No. | Ja, Nein.
yah, nine.

Please, Thank you. | Bitte, Danke.
bitt'-er, dunk'-er.

Excuse me, I am sorry. | Entschuldigen Sie, Verzeihen Sie.
ent-shōŏl -dig-en zee, fair-tsi'-en zee.

Don't mention it. | Bitte.
bitt'-er.

Pardon ? What do you say ? | Bitte ? Was sagen Sie ?
bitt'-er, vuss zahg'-en zee.

Good-morning. | Guten Morgen.
goot'-en morg'en.

Good-afternoon. | Guten Tag.
goot'en tahg.

Good-evening. | Guten Abend, Gute
Good-night. | Nacht (familiar).
goot'en ah'-bent, goot'-er naCHt.

| Good-bye. | Auf Wiedersehen. |

owf vee'-der-zay-en.

| Do you speak English? | Sprechen Sie englisch? |

shprech'-en zee eng'-lish.

| I do not speak German. | Ich spreche nicht deutsch. |

ich shprech'-er nicht doytsh.

| I do not understand. | Ich verstehe nicht. |

ich fair-shtay'-er nicht.

| Will you please speak more slowly. | Bitte sprechen Sie langsamer. |

bitt'er shprech'-en zee lung'-zahm-er.

| Write it down, please. | Bitte schreiben Sie es auf. |

bitt'-er shrī'-ben zee ez owf.

| You do not understand me. | Sie verstehen mich nicht. |

zee fair-shtay'-en mich nicht.

| What time is it? | Wie spät ist es? |

vee shpate ist ez.

| Is it time to go? | Ist es Zeit zu gehen? |

ist ez tsite tsoo gay'-en.

| I must go. | Ich muss gehen. |

ich mŏŏss gay'-en.

| Is that clock right? | Geht diese Uhr richtig? |

gait dee'-zer oor richt'-ich.

| It is late. | Es ist spät. |

ez ist shpate.

| It is still very early. | Es ist noch sehr früh. |

ez ist noCH zair trü

| Am I interrupting you? | Störe ich? |

shtur'-rer ich.

| Are you ready? | Sind Sie fertig? |

zint zee fair'-tich.

| As soon as possible. | So bald wie möglich. |
| | zo bult vee mu*r*g'-li*ch*. |

| At the latest. | Spätestens. |
| | shpate'-est-ens. |

| Bring me —— | Bringen Sie mir —— |
| | bring'-en zee mere. |

| Come here ! | Kommen Sie her ! |
| | komm'-en zee hair. |

| Come in ! | Herein ! |
| | hair-ine' |

| Do what I tell you. | Tun Sie, was ich Ihnen sage. |
| | toon zee, vuss i*ch* ee'nen zah*g*'-er. |

| Don't do that. | Tun Sie das nicht. |
| | toon zee duss ni*ch*t. |

| Don't trouble yourself. | Bemühen Sie sich nicht. |
| | be*r*-mü'-en zee zi*ch* ni*ch*t. |

| Don't forget. | Vergessen Sie nicht. |
| | fair-guess'-en zee ni*ch*t. |

| Hardly ever. | Kaum. |
| | kowm |

| Have the kindness | Haben Sie die Güte. |
| | hah'-ben zee dee gü'-te*r*. |

| How long must I wait ? | Wie lange muss ich warten? |
| | vee lung'-e*r* moöss i*ch* va*r*'-ten. |

| How much ? | Wie viel ? |
| | vee feel. |

| How soon, when ? | Wann ? |
| | vunn. |

| I am busy. | Ich bin beschäftigt. |
| | i*ch* bin besh-eft'-i*ch*t. |

| I am hot, cold. | Mir ist warm, kalt. |
| | mere ist va*r*-m, kult. |

| I am hungry, thirsty. | Ich habe Hunger, Durst. |
| | i*ch* hah'-be*r* hoöng'-e*r*, doörst. |

I am tired, sleepy.	Ich bin müde, schläfrig.

ich bin mü'-de*r*, shlay'-fri*ch*.

I am glad.	Ich freue mich.

ich froy'-e*r* mi*ch*.

I am very sorry.	Ich bedauere sehr.

ich bed-ow'-er-e*r* zair.

I am very angry.	Ich bin sehr böse.

ich bin zair bur'-zer.

I believe so.	Ich glaube.

ich glow'-be*r*.

I don't believe it.	Ich glaube es nicht.

ich glow'-be*r* ez ni*ch*t.

I don't know.	Ich weiss nicht.

ich vice ni*ch*t.

I know.	Ich weiss.

ich vice.

I see !	Ach so !

a*CH* zo.

I don't want it.	Nein danke.

nine dunk'e*r*.

I have lost.	Ich habe verloren.

ich hah'-be*r* fair-lo'-ren.

I hope.	Ich hoffe.

ich hoff'-e*r*.

I insist upon it.	Ich bestehe darauf.

i*ch* besh-tay'-e*r* dar-owf'.

I promise you.	Ich verspreche Ihnen.

ich fair-shpre*ch*-e*r* ee'-nen.

Is it not so ?	Nicht wahr ?

ni*ch*t var.

I will give you my address.	Ich gebe Ihnen meine Adresse.

ich gay'-be*r* ee'-nen mī'-ne*r* ad-dress'-e*r*.

Let us go for a walk.	Gehen wir spazieren.

gay'-en vere shput-tseer'-en.

Listen to me.	Hören Sie.
	hur'-ren zee.
Look out !	Passen Sie auf !
	pus'-sen zee owf.
More or less.	Mehr oder weniger.
	mair ō'-der vay'-nig-er.
Not so fast.	Nicht so schnell.
	nicht zo shnell.
Open the door.	Machen Sie die Tür auf.
	maCH'-en zee dee tür owf.
Shut the window.	Schliessen Sie das Fenster.
	shleess'-en zee duss fen'-ster.
Please can you tell me ?	Bitte, können Sie mir sagen ?
	bitt'-er, kurn'-en zee mere zahg'-en.
Please repeat.	Bitte wiederholen Sie.
	bitt'-er vee-der-ho'-len zee.
Speak to him.	Sprechen Sie mit ihm.
	shprech'-en zee mit eem.
Tell him to wait.	Lassen Sie ihn warten.
	luss'-en zee een var'-ten.
Wait a minute, please.	Bitte, warten Sie einen Moment.
	bitt'-er, var'-ten zee i'nen mo-ment'.
Wait for us.	Warten Sie auf uns.
	var'-ten zee owf ōōns.
We are in a hurry.	Wir haben es eilig.
	vere hah'-ben ez i'-lich.
We are much obliged to you.	Wir sind Ihnen sehr verbunden.
	vere zint ee'-nen zair fair-bōōnd'-en.
What ?	Wie bitte ?
	vee bitt'-er.

| What does that mean ? | Was bedeutet das ? |
| | vuss be-doi'tet duss. |

| What have I to pay ? | Was muss ich zahlen ? |
| | vuss mōoss ich tsah'-len. |

| What is that for ? | Wofür ist das ? |
| | vo-für' ist duss. |

| What is that in German ? | Wie heisst das auf deutsch ? |
| | vee hisst duss owf doytsh. |

| What is the matter ? | Was ist los ? |
| | vuss ist loce. |

| What is your name ? | Wie heissen Sie ? |
| | vee hiss'-en zee. |

| What is your address ? | Wo wohnen Sie ? |
| | vo vo'-nen zee. |

| Where ? | Wo ? |
| | vo. |

| Where are you going ? | Wohin gehen Sie ? |
| | vo-hin' gay'en zee. |

| Who, Who is it ? | Wer, Wer ist das ? |
| | vair, vair ist duss. |

| Who is knocking ? | Wer klopft ? |
| | vair klopft. |

| Why, Why not ? | Warum, Warum nicht ? |
| | var-ōom', var-ōom' nicht. |

| Will you come with me ? | Wollen Sie mit mir kommen ? |
| | voll'-en zee mit mere komm'-en. |

| Where can I wash my hands ? | Wo kann ich mir die Hände waschen ? |
| | vo kun ich mere dee hend'-er vush'-en. |

| Where is the W.C. ? | Wo ist die Toilette ? |
| | vo ist dee twa-lett'-er. |

| Where is the British Consulate ? | Wo ist das englische Konsulat ? |

vo ist duss eng'-lish-e*r* kon-zool-aht'

| Where is the Police Office ? | Wo ist das Polizei-Amt ? |

vo ist duss pol-eet-sī'-umt.

| Where is the Post Office ? | Wo ist das Postamt ? |

vo ist duss posst'-umt.

WRITING LETTERS

The address should be written and grouped as follows : (The three alternative words at the beginning mean " Mr., Mrs., Miss.")

Herr, Frau, Fräulein, X., Berlin, S.W.1, York Str. 100.

The usual ways of beginning and ending a private letter are :

Dear Sir.	Sehr geehrter Herr.
Dear Mr. X.	Sehr geehrter Herr X.
Dear Madam.	Sehr geehrte gnädige Frau.
Dear Mrs. X.	Sehr geehrte Frau X.
Yours truly.	Hochachtungsvoll (mainly in business letters).
Yours faithfully.	Ihr ergebener.
Yours sincerely.	Ihr.

In commercial correspondence, the firm's name only is written at the head of the letter, which begins without further preface.

Additional phrases :

With best wishes.	Mit bestem Gruss.
With kind regards.	Mit freundlichen Grüssen.
With love.	Mit herzlichen Grüssen.
Remember me to ——	Empfehlen Sie mich——
Give my love to ——	grüssen Sie ——

TELEPHONING

Numbers are pronounced in twos, e.g. 504185 *would be Fünfzig-einundvierzig fünfundachzig. The figure two is often pronounced zwo (tsvo) instead of* zwei, *to save confusion with* drei.

I want to telephone.	Ich möchte telephonieren.

ich mur*ch*'-te*r* tel-e*r*-phone-eer'-en.

Who is speaking?	Wer ist da?

vair ist dah.

This is ——	Hier ist ——

here ist.

Can I speak to——?	Kann ich —— sprechen?

kun i*ch*—shpre*ch*'-en.

A telephone call.	Ein Anruf.

ine un'-roof.

Telephone, Call-box.	Fernsprecher, Münzfernsprecher.

fairn'-shpre*ch*-er, münts'-fairn-shpre*ch*-er.

Operator.	Fräulein.

froy'-line.

Wrong number.	Falsche Verbindung.

fulsh'-e*r* fair-bin'-dŏong.

Will you get me the number?	Bitte, verbinden Sie mich.

bitt'-e*r*, fair-bin'-den zee mi*ch*.

Ring me up.	Rufen Sie mich an.

roof'-en zee mi*ch* un.

I shall ring up later.	Ich werde später anrufen.

i*ch* vair'-de*r* shpay'-te*r* un'-roof-en.

Trunk-call.	Ferngespräch.

fairn'-gesh-pre*ch*.

TRAVELLING BY TRAIN

ARRIVING

When do we arrive at the frontier ? | Wann kommen wir an die Grenze ?
vun komm'-en vere un dee grents'-er.

What station is this ? | Wie heisst dieser Bahnhof ?
vee hīsst dee'-zer bahn'-hōf.

How long does the train stop ? | Wie lange hält der Zug ?
vee lung'-er helt dair tsoog.

Can I get out ? | Kann ich aussteigen ?
kun ich owce'-shtī-gen.

Can I break the journey ? | Kann ich die Reise unterbrechen ?
kun ich dee rī'-zer ŏŏn-ter-brech'-en.

Have I time to go to the refreshment room ? | Habe ich Zeit, in den Speisesaal zu gehen ?
hah'-ber ich tsite, in dane shpī'-zer-zahl tsoo gay'-en.

Where is the refreshment room ? | Wo ist der Speisesaal ?
vo ist dair shpī'-zer-zahl.

Two cups of coffee, please. | Zwei Tassen Kaffee bitte.
tsvī tuss'-en kuff'-ay bitt'-er.

Is the train late ? | Hat der Zug Verspätung ?
hut dair tsoog fair-shpate'-ŏŏng.

Tickets, please. | Fahrkarten bitte.
far'-kart-en bitt'-er.

I want a taxi. | Ich möchte einen Taxi haben.
ich murcht'-er ī'-nen tux'-e hah'. ben.

26

| Call me a taxi. | Holen Sie mir einen Taxi. |
| | *ho'-len zee mere i'-nen tux'-e.* |

| Where are the taxis ? | Wo sind die Taxis ? |
| | *vo zint dee tux'-eez.* |

| Is there a hotel bus here ? | Ist ein Wagen vom Hotel hier ? |
| | *ist ine vah'-gen fom ho-tell' here.* |

| I will go by the hotel bus. | Ich nehme den Hotel-wagen. |
| | *ich nay'-mer dane ho-tell'-vah-gen.* |

| How far is it ? | Wie weit ist es ? |
| | *vee vite ist ez.* |

CHANGING

| Must I change trains ? | Muss ich umsteigen ? |
| | *mŏŏss ich ŏŏm'-shtī-gen.* |

| Where must I change ? | Wo muss ich umsteigen ? |
| | *vo mŏŏss ich ŏŏm'-shtī-gen.* |

| Where is the best place to change ? | Wo steige ich am besten um ? |
| | *vo shtī'-ger ich um best'-en ŏŏm.* |

| Where does the other train go from ? | Wo fährt der andere Zug ab ? |
| | *vo fairt dair un'-der-er tsoog up.* |

| Does the train go from a different station ? | Fährt der Zug von einem anderen Bahnhof ab ? |
| | *fairt dair tsoog fon i'-nem un'-der-en bahn'-hōf up.* |

| When does the train go ? | Wann fährt der Zug ? |
| | *vunn fairt dair tsoog.* |

| Is there an immediate connection ? | Habe ich direkten Anschluss ? |
| | *hah'-ber ich dee-rect'-en un'-shlŏŏss.* |

| Is it a through train to——? | Fährt der Zug nach —— durch ? |
| | *fairt dair tsoog naCH—doorch.* |

How long have I to wait ?	Wie lange muss ich warten ?

vee lung'-er mŏoss ich vart'-en.

Have I time to see the town ?	Habe ich Zeit, die Stadt zu besichtigen ?

hah'-ber ich tsite, dee shtutt tsoo bez-ich'-tig-en.

Does the train go to——?	Fährt der Zug nach——?

fairt dair tsoog naCH——

Does the train pass through——?	Fährt der Zug über——?

fairt dair tsoog ü'-ber——

Does the train stop at——?	Hält der Zug in——?

helt dair tsoog in——

Is the train in ?	Ist der Zug schon da ?

ist dair tsoog shōn dah.

Is the train busy ?	Ist der Zug voll ?

ist dair tsoog foll.

DEPARTING

Where is the main station ?	Wo ist der Hauptbahn-hof ?

vo ist dair howpt'-bahn-hŏf.

Which way is the station for——?	Wie komme ich zum Bahnhof nach——?

vee komm'-er ich tsŏom bahn'-hŏf nach——

When does the train for —— go ?	Wann fährt der Zug für —— ab ?

vunn fairt dair tsoog für—up.

Which is the way to the trains ?	Wie komme ich zu den Zügen ?

vee komm'-er ich tsoo dane tsü'-gen.

Which platform does the train go from ?	Von welchem Bahnsteig fährt der Zug ab ?

fon vellch'-em bahn'-shtīg fairt der tsoog up.

Is it an express ?	Ist es ein Schnellzug ?

ist ez ine shnell'-tsoog.

Is there a supplementary charge ?	Muss ich Zuschlag zahlen ?

moŏss ich tsoo'-shlahg tsah'-len.

How much is the supplement ?	Wie hoch ist der Zuschlag ?

vee hōCH ist dair tsoo'-shlahg.

Is that valid for an express ?	Gilt das für Schnellzüge ?

gilt duss für shnell'-tsüg'-er.

Is there a first, second class ?	Hat der Zug erste, zweite Klasse ?

hut lair tsoog airst'-er, tsvī'-ter, kluss'-er.

Is there a dining-car, sleeping-car on the train?	Hat der Zug Speise-wagen, Schlafwagen ?

hut dair tsoog shpī'-zer vah-gen, shlahf'-vah-gen.

Is there a second class sleeping-car ?	Gibt es Schlafwagen zweiter Klasse ?

geebt ez shlahf'-vah-gen tsvī'-ter kluss'-er.

How much extra does it cost ?	Was kostet es extra ?

vuss kost'-et ez extra.

Must I (can I) reserve a seat ?	Muss ich (kann ich) einen Platz belegen ?

moŏss ich (kunn ich) ī'-nen pluts ber-lay'-gen.

I want a smoking (non-smoking) compartment.	Ich möchte ein Raucher (Nichtraucher) Abteil.

ich murch'-ter ine rowCH'-er (nicht'-rowCH'-er) up'-tile.

Is there a compartment for ladies only ?	Hat der Zug ein Frauen-Abteil ?

hut dair tsoog ine frow'-en up'-tile.

Which end of the train is it ?	An welchem Ende des Zuges ist es ?

un velch'-em end'-er dez tsoo-gez ist ez.

Are there any seats, berths, left ?	Gibt es noch Plätze, Betten ?

geebt ez noCH plet'-ser, bet'-en.

I will go and get a seat in the train.	Ich werde einen Platz im Zug belegen.

ich vair'-der ī'-nen pluts im tsoog be-lay'-gen.

Where is the booking-office ?	Wo ist die Fahrkar-tenausgabe ?

vo ist dee far'-kart-en-owce'-gahb-er.

First (2nd) class return to Hamburg.	Hamburg hin und zurück, erster (zweiter) Klasse.

hum'-boorg hin ŏont tsŏo-rük'airst'-er (tsvi'-ter) kluss'-er.

Two singles to Cologne.	Köln zweimal.

kurln tsvī'-mahl.

Single ticket.	Einfache Fahrkarte.

ine'-faCH-er far'-kart-er.

Return ticket.	Rückfahrkarte.

rük'-far-kart-er.

Please write down the price.	Bitte, schreiben Sie den Preis auf.

bitt'-er, shrī'-ben zee dane price owf.

Where can I get a plat-form ticket ?	Wo bekommt man Bahnsteigkarten ?

vo bek-ommt' mun bahn'-shtīg-kart-en.

Which way does the train go ?	In welcher Richtung fährt der Zug ?

in vellch'-er richt'-ŏong fairt dair tsoog.

Where is the guard, attendant ?	Wo ist der Zugführer, Kondukteur ?

vo ist dair tsoog'-für-er, kon-dook-tur.

Will the train be crowded ?	Wird der Zug voll sein ?

virt dair tsoog foll zine.

| Can I have an upper (lower) berth ? | Kann ich ein oberes (unteres) Bett haben ? |

kun *ich* ine ŏ'-ber-ez (ŏŏnt'-er-ez) bet hah'-ben.

| We want to be alone if possible. | Wir möchten möglichst allein sein. |

vere mu*r*cht'-en mu*r*g'-lich*s*t al-ine' zine.

| Can I get —— on the train ? | Kann ich —— im Zug bekommen ? |

kun *ich*—im tsoog bek-omm'-en.

| I want a pillow, rug. | Ich möchte ein Kissen (eine Decke). |

ich mu*r*cht'- e*r* ine kiss'-en, ĭ'-ne*r* deck'-e*r*.

| What time is breakfast, lunch, tea, dinner ? | Wann gibt es Frühstück, Mittagessen, Tee, Abendessen ? |

vun geebt ez frü-shtük, mitt'-ahg-ess-en, tay, ah'-bent-ess-en.

| When do we arrive ? | Wann kommen wir an ? |

vun komm'-en vere un.

| Wake me at—— | Wecken Sie mich um—— |

veck'-en zee mi*ch* ŏŏm——

| Bring me a cup of tea, coffee in the morning. | Bringen Sie mir eine Tasse Tee, Kaffee, am Morgen. |

bring'-en zee mere ĭ'-ne*r* tuss'-e*r* tay, kuff'-ay, um morg'-en.

| I should like some hot water. | Ich möchte etwas warmes Wasser. |

ich mu*r*cht'-e*r* et'-vuss varm'-ez vuss'-er.

AT THE STATION, LUGGAGE

Luggage can be registered for a moderate charge. It is given up at the station of departure, and the traveller need not have anythng more to do with it till he collects it on arrival at his destination.   Theoretically, this is the ideal way of dealing with luggage, especially with large pieces, but under present conditions the traveller is well advised to keep an eye on his luggage, even at the cost of a little extra trouble with porters, etc.

Porter !	Träger !
	tray'-ger.
Please take my luggage.	Bitte nehmen Sie mein Gepäck.
	bitt'-er nay'-men zee mine gep-eck'.
Can you carry the other case too ?	Können Sie den zweiten Koffer auch tragen ?
	kurn'-en zee dane tsvī'-ten koff'-er owCH trahg'-en.
I have a lot of luggage.	Ich habe viel Gepäck.
	ich hah'-ber feel gep-eck'.
I have some big luggage too.	Ich habe auch grosses Gepäck.
	ich hah'-ber owCH grōs'-ez gep-eck'.
Four pieces.	Vier Stück.
	feer shtük.
Where is the luggage van ?	Wo ist der Gepäck-wagen ?
	vo ist dair gep-eck'-vahg'-en.
Where is the left-luggage ?	Wo ist der Handgepäck-schalter ?
	vo ist dair hunt'-gep-eck-shull'-ter.

(*See also pp*. 34-36).

Where do I register my luggage ?	Wo gebe ich mein Gepäck auf ?
	vo gay'-ber ich mine gep-eck' owf.

Can I take these three bags in the compartment with me?	Kann ich diese drei Koffer ins Abteil mitnehmen?

kun ich dee'-zer dry koff'-er ins up'-tile mit'-nay-men.

| I will register my trunk. | Ich werde meinen grossen Koffer aufgeben. |

ich vair'-der mī'-nen grōs'-en koff'-er owf'-gay-ben.

| Please register these pieces for me. | Bitte geben Sie diese Stücke für mich auf. |

bitt'-er gay'-ben zee dee'-zer shtük'-er für mich owf.

| I want to send these bags through to—— | Ich möchte diese Koffer direkt nach —— senden. |

ich murch'-ter dee'-zer koff'-er dee-rect' naCH—zen'-den.

| Are they certain to be there when I arrive? | Werden sie bestimmt da sein, wenn ich ankomme? |

vair'-den zee besh-timmt' dah zine venn ich un'-komm-er.

| Have I time to register my trunk? | Habe ich Zeit, meinen grossen Koffer aufzugeben? |

hah'-ber ich tsite, mī'-nen grōs'-en koff'-er owf'-tsoo-gay-ben.

| Register my luggage and bring me the slip back quickly. | Geben Sie mein Gepäck auf und bringen Sie mir schnell den Schein. |

gay'-ben zee mine gep-eck' owf ŏŏnt bring'-en zee mere shnell dane shine.

| I want to insure my luggage. | Ich will mein Gepäck versichern. |

ich vill mine gep-eck' fair-zich'-ern.

G.   B

| What will it cost to insure the trunk? | Was kostet es, den grossen Koffer zu versichern? |

vuss kost'-et ez, dane grōs'-en koff'-er tsoo fair-zich'-ern.

| It is not worth while. | Es lohnt sich nicht. |

ez loant zich nicht.

| Here is the luggage-slip. | Hier ist der Gepäckschein. |

here ist dair gep-eck'-shine.

| Will you fetch it? | Wollen Sie es holen? |

voll'-en zee ez hō'-len.

| Must I come too? | Muss ich mitkommen? |

mŏoss ich mit'-komm-en.

| Where shall I find you? | Wo werde ich Sie treffen? |

vo vair'-der ich zee treff'-en.

| Wait for me here. | Warten Sie hier auf mich. |

var'-ten zee here owf mich.

| I am going to the buffet; where shall I find you again? | Ich gehe zum Buffet; wo finde ich Sie wieder? |

ich gay'-er tsŏom büf-ay'; vo fin'-der ich zee vee'-der.

| I shall meet you on the platform. | Ich treffe Sie am Bahnsteig. |

ich treff'-er zee um bahn'-shtīg.

AT THE LEFT-LUGGAGE

(Handgepäck)

| I wish to leave these things here. | Ich will diese Sachen hier lassen. |

ich vill dee'-zer zaCH'-en here luss'-en.

| Three suitcases, an over-coat, a rug, this parcel and these books ; also my umbrella. | Drei Handkoffer, ein Mantel, eine Decke, dieses Paket und diese Bücher ; auch mein Regenschirm. |

dry hunt'-koff-er, ine mun'-tel, i'-ner deck'-er, dee'-zez puck-ate' öont dee'-zer büch'-er ; owCH mine ray'-gen-shirm.

| Please do it quickly. | Bitte machen Sie schnell. |

bitt'-er maCH'-en zee shnell.

| There is one suitcase missing. | Es fehlt ein Handkoffer. |

ez failt ine hunt'-koff-er.

| Where is my umbrella ? | Wo ist mein Schirm ? |

vo ist mine shirm.

| That is mine over there. | Das ist meins, da drüben |

duss ist mīnss, dah drü'-ben.

| These are not mine. | Die sind nicht meine Sachen. |

dee zint nicht mi'-ner zaCH'-en.

| I want to take out one case. | Ich möchte einen Koffer mitnehmen. |

ich murch'-ter i'-nen koff'-er mit'-nay-men.

| Can I still leave the rest here ? | Kann ich die andern Sachen noch hier lassen ? |

kun ich dee un'-dern zaCH'-en noCH here luss'-en.

| Give me another slip. | Geben Sie mir einen neuen Schein. |

gay'-ben zee mere i'-nen noy'-en shine.

| How much is there to pay ? | Was kostet es ? |

vuss kost'-et ez.

| How much do you charge for each ? | Was kostet das Stück ? |

vuss kost'-et duss shtük.

Do these count as one?	Gilt das als ein Stück?

guilt duss als ine shtük.

| Do I pay now, or when I collect the things? | Soll ich jetzt zahlen, oder wenn ich die Sachen abhole? |

zoll ich yetst tsahl'-en ō'-der venn ich dee zaCH'-en up'-hō-ler.

| The one case is not locked. | Der eine Koffer ist nicht verschlossen. |

dair ī'-ner koff'-er ist nicht fair-shloss'-en.

| The catch is broken, I cannot shut it. | Der Verschluss ist kaputt; ich kann ihn nicht zumachen. |

dair fair-shloos' ist ku-pōōt'; ich kunn een nicht tsoo'-maCH-en.

| Does it matter? | Macht es etwas aus? |

maCHt ez et'-vuss owce.

| Something has dropped out. | Es ist etwas herausge-fallen. |

ez ist et'-vuss hair-owce'-gef-al-en.

| Is there a porter here to take my things? | Ist ein Träger hier, der meine Sachen nehmen kann? |

ist ine tray'-ger here, dair mī'-ner zaCH'-en nay'-men kunn.

| Please keep an eye on my things till I find a porter. | Bitte passen Sie auf meine Sachen auf, bis ich einen Träger finde. |

bitt'-er pus'-en zee owf mi'-ner zaCH'-en owf biss ich ī'-nen tray'-ger fin'-der.

| I shall be back about six; I am going to have a look round the town for a couple of hours. | Ich komme gegen sechs Uhr zurück; ich gehe für ein paar Stunden in die Stadt. |

ich komm'-er gay'-gen zex oor tsoo-rük'; ich gay'-er für ine par shtōōn'-den in dee shtutt.

AT THE STATION, GENERAL

Arrival platform, Departure.	Ankunftsbahnsteig, Abfahrt.

un'-kŏonfts-bahn-shtīg, up'-fart.

Booking Office, Enquiry Office.	Fahrkartenausgabe, Auskunftsstelle.

far'-kart-en-owce-gahb-er, owce'-kŏonfts-shtell-er.

Lost Property Office.	Fundbüro.

fŏont'-bü-ro.

First-aid post, Railway Police.	Sanitätswache, Bahnhofspolizei.

zun-it-aits'-vaCH-er, bahn'-hŏfs-pol-ee-tsī.

Stationmaster.	Bahnhofsvorsteher.

bahn'-hŏfs-fore-shtay-er.

Railway official.	Bahnhofsbeamter.

bahn'-hŏfs-bay-umt-er.

Waiting-room.	Wartesaal.

vart'-er-zahl.

Ladies' room, Gentlemen.	Damen, Herren.

dah'-men, hair'-en.

Can you change me some money ?	Können Sie mir Geld wechseln ?

kurn'-en zee mere gelt vex'-eln.

Bookstall.	Buchhandlung.

booCH'-hunt-lŏong.

Have you any English papers, books ?	Haben Sie englische Zeitungen, Bücher ?

hah'-ben zee eng'-lish-er tsī'-tŏong-en, büch'-er.

These are old.	Diese sind alt.

dee'-zer zint ult.

Where can I post a letter ?	Wo kann ich einen Brief einwerfen ?

vo kunn ich ī'-nen brief ine'-verf-en.

| Have you any post-cards (picture post-cards) ? | Haben Sie Postkarten, Ansichtskarten ? |

hah'-ben zee post'-kart-en, un'-zichts-kart-en.

| Where can I get stamps ? | Wo bekommt man Briefmarken ? |

vo bek-ommt mun brief'-mark-en.

| Where can I send a tele-gram ? | We kann ich ein Tele-gramm abschicken ? |

vo kunn ich ine tel-eg-rum' up'-shick-en.

TIME-TABLES

Local railway guides may be obtained at moderate prices. In Germany it is as well to inquire at the station or consult the large time-tables which are posted up in all the stations, to con-firm times of trains. The various travel agencies are also reliable sources of information, both for internal and international train services. Arrival times given for international trains should be verified to make sure that they represent local time at the destination.

| I want a time-table. | Ich möchte einen Fahrplan. |

ich murch'-ter i'-nen far'-plun.

| Does this section include——? | Steht in diesem Band auch——? |

shtate in dee'-zem bunt owCH——

| Does this give the trains to —— as well as to ——? | Sind hier die Züge nach —— und die Züge nach —— drin ? |

zint here dee tsü'-ger naCH——ŏŏnt dee tsü'-ger naCH
——drin.

| Then give me these two sections. | Dann geben Sie mir diese beiden Hefte. |

dunn gay'-ben zee mere dee'-zer bi'-den heft'-er.

| This will do. | Es ist gut so. |
| | ez ist goot zo. |

| Can you show me how to use this time-table ? | Können Sie mir bitte diesen Fahrplan erklären ? |
| kurn'-en zee mere bitt'-er dee'-zen far'-plahn air-klair'-en. | |

| What does this stand for ? | Was bedeutet dieses Zeichen ? |
| vuss bed-oyt'-et dee'-zez tsich'-en. | |

ON THE TRAIN

| I should like a corner seat (window seat). | Ich möchte einen Ecksitz (Fenstersitz) haben. |
| ich murch'-ter i'-nen eck'-zits (fen'-ster-zits) hah'-ben. | |

| Facing (back to) the engine. | Vorwärts (Rückwärts). |
| for'-vairts (rük'-vairts). | |

| Is this seat free ? | Ist dieser Platz frei ? |
| ist dee'-zer pluts fry. | |

| That seat is taken. | Der Platz ist besetzt. |
| dair pluts ist bez-etst'. | |

| Put my luggage on the rack (under the seat). | Legen Sie mein Gepäck ins Netz (unter die Bank). |
| lay'-gen zee mine gep-eck' inz nets (ŏŏn'-ter dee bunk). | |

| May I get past, please ? | Darf ich bitte vorbeikommen ? |
| darf ich bitt'-er for-by'-komm-en. | |

| Can you make room, please ? | Wollen Sie bitte Platz machen ? |
| voll'-en zee bitt'-er pluts maCH'-en. | |

| I am sorry to disturb you. | Verzeihen Sie die Störung. |
| fair-tsi'-en zee dee shtur'-rŏŏng. | |

Perhaps you would let us sit together?	Würden Sie uns zusammen sitzen lassen?

vür'-den zee ōōns tsōō-zamm'-en zits'-en luss'-en.

Are my feet in your way?	Sind meine Füsse im Wege?

zint mī'-ner füss'-er im vay'-ger.

Not in the least.	Nicht im geringsten.

nicht im ger-ing'-sten.

It's quite all right.	Bitte schön.

bitt'-er schurn.

Do you mind if I smoke?	Stört es Sie, wenn ich rauche?

shturt ez zee, venn ich rowCH-er.

Excuse me! I can't bear tobacco smoke.	Verzeihen Sie! Ich kann keinen Rauch vertragen.

fair-tsī-en zee'! ich kun kī'-nen rowCH fair-trahg'-en.

This is a non-smoking compartment.	Dies ist ein Nichtraucher-abteil.

deess ist ine nicht'-rowCH'-er-up'-tile.

Can you give me a light, please?	Können Sie mir bitte Feuer geben?

kurn'-en zee mere bitt'-er foy'-er gay'-ben.

May I borrow your newspaper?	Darf ich Ihre Zeitung sehen?

darf ich ee'-rer tsī'-tōong zay'-en.

Would you like to look at my paper?	Möchten Sie meine Zeitung sehen?

murch'-ten zee mī'-ner tsī'-tōong zay'-en.

May I open the window?	Darf ich das Fenster aufmachen?

darf ich duss fen'-ster owt'-maCH-en.

Would you shut the window?	Würden Sie das Fenster zumachen?

vür'-den zee duss fen'-ster tsoo'-maCH-en.

| The window does not open. | Das Fenster geht nicht auf. |

duss fen'-ster gate nicht owf.

| The door is jammed. | Die Tür sperrt sich. |

dee tür sperrt sich.

| It is hot (cold). | Es ist warm (kalt). |

ez ist varm (kult).

| The heating is on. | Die Heizung ist angestellt. |

dee hī'-tsŏong ist un'-gesh-tellt.

| There is a draught here. | Es zieht hier. |

ez tseet here.

| Do you feel a draught ? | Zieht es Ihnen ? |

tseet ez ee'-nen.

| Please put on the light. | Bitte, machen Sie Licht. |

bitt'-er maCH'-en zee licht.

| Is the sun troubling you ? | Stört Sie die Sonne ? |

shturt zee dee zonn'-er.

| Please pull down the blind. | Bitte ziehen Sie den Vorhang zu. |

bitt'-er tsee'-en zee dane fore'-hung tsoo.

| Where is the bell for the attendant ? | Wo ist die Klingel für den Kellner ? |

vo ist dee kling'-el für dane kell'-ner.

| I want something to drink. | Ich möchte etwas zu trinken. |

ich murch'-ter et'-vuss tsoo trink'-en.

| Are we nearly there ? | Sind wir bald da ? |

zint vere bult dah.

| How much longer is it ? | Wie lange dauert es noch ? |

vee lung'-er dow'-ert ez noCH.

| What are we stopping for ? | Warum halten wir ? |

var-ŏom' hult'-en vere.

We are very late.	Wir haben viel Verspätung.

vere hah'-ben feel fair-shpate'-ŏŏng.

We are on time.	Wir haben keine Verspätung.

vere hah'-ben kĭ'-ner fair-shpate'-ŏŏng.

Whereabouts are we ?	Wo sind wir jetzt ?

vo zint vere yetst.

Is that near——?	Ist das in der Nähe von——?

ist duss in dair nay'-er fon——

Do you know if we pass through——?	Wissen Zie, ob wir über —— fahren ?

viss'-en zee, op vere über—far'-en.

Somebody is sitting in my place.	Jemand sitzt auf meinem Platz.

yay'-munt zitst owf mĭ'-nem pluts.

Here is my ticket.	Hier ist meine Fahrkarte.

here ist mĭ'-ner far'-kar-ter.

Where is the communication cord ?	Wo ist die Notbremse ?

vo ist dee note'-brem-zer.

TRAVELLING BY BOAT

When does the steamer start ?	Wann fährt der Dampfer ?

vunn fairt dair dump'-fer.

| Where do I get tickets ? | Wo bekomme ich Fahrkarten ? |

vo ber-komm'-er ich far'-kar-ten.

| Two tickets for ——, please. | Zwei Karten nach —— bitte. |

tsvī kar'-ten naCH—bitt'-er.

| Is there room third class ? | Ist in der dritten Klasse noch Platz ? |

ist in dair dritt'-en kluss'-er noCH pluts.

| Is there an upper deck ? | Gibt es ein Promenadendeck ? |

geebt ez ine prom-en-ahd'-en-deck.

| Can I have meals on board ? | Kann ich an Bord essen ? |

kunn ich un bort ess'-en.

| Can I land at——? | Kann ich in —— landen ? |

kunn ich in—lun'-den.

| Can I have a deck cabin ? | Kann ich eine Deckkabine haben ? |

kunn ich ī'-ner deck-ka-bee'-ner hah'-ben.

| Will you show me my cabin ? | Würden Sie mir meine Kabine zeigen ? |

vür'-den zee mere mī'-ner ka-bee'-ner tsī'-gen.

| Can I see the other one ? | Darf ich die andere sehen ? |

darf ich dee un'-der-er zay'-en.

May I change my berth ?	Kann ich meine Kabine wechseln ?

kunn i*ch* mī'-ne*r* ka-bee'-ne*r* vex'-eln.

Where is the luggage put ?	Wo wird das Gepäck untergebracht ?

vo virt duss gep-eck' ŏŏn'-ter-geb-raCHt.

Which is the way on deck ?	Wo geht es zum Deck ?

vo gate ez tsŏŏm deck.

Which is the way below ?	Wo geht es hinunter ?

vo gate ez hin-ŏŏnt'-ter.

Where is the restaurant, bar ?	Wo ist das Restaurant, die Bar ?

vo ist duss rest'-or-oñ, dee bar.

Where is the —— class saloon ?	Wo ist der Salon —— Klasse ?

vo ist dair sal-oñ'—kluss'-e*r*.

Would you close the port-hole ?	Wollen Sie bitte das Fenster schliessen ?

voll'-en zee bitt'-e*r* duss fen'-ster shleess'-en.

I want a deck-chair.	Ich möchte einen Liegestuhl.

i*ch* mu*r*ch'-te*r* ĭ'-nen lee'-ge*r*-schtool.

What is the extra charge ?	Was kostet es extra ?

vuss kost'-et ez extra.

We shall have a good crossing.	Wir werden eine gute Überfahrt haben.

vere vair'-den ĭ'-ne*r* goot'-e*r* ü'-ber-fart hah'-ben.

When does the boat arrive at——?	Wann kommt das Schiff in —— an ?

vunn kommt duss shiff in—un.

Must I get a landing ticket ?	Muss ich eine Landungs- karte haben?

mŏŏss i*ch* ĭ'-ne*r* lun'-dŏŏngz-kar'-te*r* hah'-ben.

Do we need passports ?	Brauchen wir Pässe ?

browCH'-en vere pess'-er.

Are the passports examined on board ?	Werden die Pässe an Bord kontrolliert ?

vair'-den dee pess'-er un bort kon-trol-eert'.

Can I have tea in my cabin ?	Kann ich Tee in meiner Kabine haben ?

kann ich tay in mī'-ner ka-bee'-ner hah'-ben.

I feel sick.	Mir ist schlecht.

mere ist shlecht.

Please bring me a basin.	Bitte, bringen Sie mir ein Becken.

bitt'-er bring'-en zee mere ine beck'-en.

Bring me a brandy.	Bringen Sie mir bitte einen Cognac.

bring'-en zee mere bitt'-er i'-nen con'-yac.

I feel better.	Es geht mir besser.

ez gate mere bess'-er.

TRAVELLING BY AIR

Where is the air travel office?	Wo ist das Büro für Luftverkehr?

vo ist duss bü-ro' für looft'-fair-care.

Is there a plane from here to——?	Fährt ein Flugzeug von hier nach——?

fairt ine floog'-tsoyg fon here naCH——?

When does the plane leave?	Wann fährt das Flugzeug ab?

vun fairt duss floog'-tsoyg up.

When do we land in——?	Wann landen wir in——?

vun lund'-en vere in——?

Can I go direct?	Kann ich direkt fahren?

kun ich dee-rect' far'-en.

What is the fare (return)?	Was kostet es? (hin und zurück)?

vuss kost'-ət ez (hin oont tsoo-rük'.)

I want to reserve a seat in the plane leaving to-morrow morning for——	Ich möchte einen Platz in dem Flugzeug belegen, das morgen früh nach —— fährt.

ich murch'-ter ï'-nen pluts in dame floog'-tsoyg bel-ay'-gen, duss mor'-gen frü naCH—fairt.

Is the airport far from the town?	Liegt der Flughafen weit von der Stadt?

leecht dair floog'-haf-en vite fon dair shtutt.

How do I get to the aerodrome?	Wie komme ich zum Flugplatz?

vee komm'-er ich tsoom floog'-pluts.

A motor-coach leaves from outside this office at——	Ein Autobus fährt von der Tür dieses Büros um——

ine ow'-to-booss fairt fon dair tür dee'-zez bü-röz oom.

| How much luggage may I take without paying extra? | Wieviel Gepäck darf ich mitnehmen ohne zuschlag? |

vee-feel' gep-eck' darf *ich* mit'-nay-men ō'-ner tsoo'-shlag.

| What do you charge for luggage? | Was kostet das Gepäck? |

vuss kost'-et duss gep-eck'.

| How big is the plane? | Wie gross ist das Flugzeug? |

vee gross ist duss floog'-tsoyg.

| Can I have refreshments on the plane? | Kann ich im Flugzeug Erfrischungen bekommen? |

kun i*ch* im floog'-tsoyg air-frish'-ŏong-en bek-omm'-en.

| Do we land anywhere before we reach——? | Landen wir irgendwo, bevor wir nach —— kommen? |

lund'-en vere ear'-gent·vo, bef-ōr' vere naCH—komm'-en.

| Where are we now? | Wo sind wir jetzt? |

vo zint vere yetst.

| What is that river? | Was ist das für ein Fluss? |

vuss ist duss für ine flooss.

| I should like a cup of tea, coffee. | Ich hätte gern eine Tasse Tee, Kaffee. |

i*ch* hett'-er gairn ī'-ner tuss'-er tay, kuff'-ay.

| I want a rug. | Ich möchte eine Decke haben. |

i*ch* mur*ch*'-ter ī'-ner deck'-er hah'-ben.

| Can I change my seat? | Kann ich den Platz wechseln? |

kun i*ch* dane pluts vex'-eln.

| Can you open the window a bit more ? | Können Sie das Fenster etwas weiter aufmachen ? |

kurn'-en zee duss fen'-ster et'-vuss vī'-ter owf'-maCH-en.

| Do you mind if I close the window ? | Macht es Ihnen etwas aus, wenn ich das Fenster zumache ? |

maCHt ez ee'-nen et'-vuss ows, ven ich duss fen'-ster tsoo'-maCH-er.

| I feel sick. | Mir ist schlecht. |

mere ist shlecht.

| Give me a paper-bag. | Geben Sie mir eine Tüte. |

gay'-ben zee mere ī'-ner tü'-ter.

| Bring me some more. | Bringen Sie mir noch einige. |

bring'-en zee mere noCH ī'-nig-er.

| I suffer from airsickness. | Ich leide an Luftkrankheit. |

ich li'-der un looft'-krunk-hite.

| I feel better. | Es geht mir besser. |

ez gate mere bess'-er.

| Bring me a brandy, please. | Bringen Sie mir einen Cognac bitte. |

bring'-en zee mere i'-nen konn'-yak bitt'-er.

| How high are we flying ? | Wie hoch fliegen wir ? |

vee hōCH flee'-gen vere.

| Was that an air-pocket ? | War das ein Luftsack ? |

var duss ine looft'-zuck.

| It is the first time that I have travelled by plane. | Es ist das erste Mal, das ich mit dem Flugzeug fahre. |

ez ist duss airst'-er mahl duss ich mit dame floog'-tsoyg far'-er.

| Is the luggage examined at the airport ? | Wird das Gepäck am Flughafen kontrolliert ? |

virt duss gep-eck' um floog'-hah-fen kon-trol-eert'.

CUSTOMS

| Where is the Customs ? | Wo ist das Zollamt ? |

vo ist duss tsoll'-umt.

| Where is the hand-luggage (big luggage) examined ? | Wo wird das Handgepäck (grosses Gepäck) kontrolliert ? |

vo virt duss hunt'-gep eck (grōs'-ser gep-eck') kon-trol-eert'.

| Do we have to leave the train ? | Müssen wir aussteigen ? |

müss'-en vere owce'-shtī-gen.

| Where are passports examined ? | Wo werden die Pässe kontrolliert ? |

vo vair'-den dee pess'-er kon-trol-eert'.

| Here is my passport. | Hier ist mein Pass. |

here ist mine pus.

| I have £5 for the journey. | Ich habe fünf Pfund für die Reise. |

ich hah'-ber fünf pfoont für dee rī'-zer.

| I have a letter of credit for £50. | Ich habe einen Kreditbrief für fünfzig Pfund. |

ich hah'-ber ī'-nen cred-eet'-brief für fünf'-tsich pfoont.

| I have £50 in travellers' cheques. | Ich habe fünfzig Pfund Reiseschecks. |

ich hah'-ber fünf'-tsich pfoont rī'-zer-shecks.

| I have only 10 German Marks. | Ich habe nur zehn D-Mark. |

ich hah'-ber noor tsain day'-mark.

I have no Dutch, French money.	Ich habe kein holländisches, französisches Geld.

ich hah′ber kine holl-end′-ish-ez, frun-tsur′-zish-ez gelt.

I have shown my passport.	Ich habe meinen Pass gezeigt.

ich hah′-ber mī′-nen pus ger-tsīgt′.

I was waiting for the officer.	Ich habe auf den Beamten gewartet.

ich hah′-ber owf dane bay-umt′-en gev-art′-et.

Will you examine my luggage, please?	Wollen Sie bitte mein Gepäck prüfen?

voll′-en zee bitt′-er mine gep-eck′ prü′-fen.

These are all mine.	Diese gehören alle mir.

dee -zer ge-hur′-ren ull′-er mere.

Shall I open this?	Soll ich dies aufmachen?

zol ich deess owf′-maCH-en.

Must I open everything?	Muss ich alles aufmachen?

mŏŏss ich ull′-ez owf′-maCH-en.

I have nothing to declare.	Ich habe nichts zu verzollen.

ich hah′-ber nichts tsoo fair-tsol′-en.

They are for my own personal use.	Sie sind für meinen persönlichen Gebrauch.

zee zint für mī′-nen pair-zurn′-lich-en geb-rowCH′.

I am staying only a few days.	Ich bleibe nur einige Tage hier.

ich blī′-ber noor ī′-nig-er tahg′-er here.

I am not stopping in the country.	Ich halte mich in diesem Lande nicht auf.

ich hult′-er mich in dee′-zem lund′-er nicht owf.

I am travelling direct to——	Ich fahre direkt nach——

ich far′-er dee-rect′ naCH——

My trunk is heavy because it is full of books.	Mein Koffer ist schwer, weil viele Bücher darin sind.

mine koff'-er ist shvair, vile feel'-er büch'-er dar-in' zint.

I have not bought anything during my stay.	Ich habe während meines Aufenthaltes nichts gekauft.

ich hah'-ber vay'-rent mī'-nez owf'-ent-hult-ez nichts gek-owft'

They are all old.	Sie sind alle alt.

zee zint ull'-er ult.

It has been used.	Es ist gebraucht.

ez ist geb-rowCHt'.

I have worn it a lot.	Ich habe es viel getragen.

ich hah'-ber ez feel get-rahg'-en.

Please be careful.	Bitte seien Sie vorsichtig.

bitt'-er zī'-en zee fore'-zich-tich.

There is nothing dutiable underneath.	Es ist nichts Zollbares darunter.

ez ist nichts tsol'-bar-ez dar-ōōn'-ter.

Are these things dutiable ?	Sind diese Sachen verzollbar ?

zint dee'-zer zaCH'-en fair-tsol'-bar.

I do not know.	Ich weiss es nicht.

ich vice ez nicht.

How much must I pay ?	Wie viel muss ich zahlen ?

vee feel mōōss ich tsahl'-en.

I am only on holiday.	Ich bin nur auf Ferien.

ich bin noor owf fay'-ree-en.

It is a business visit.	Es ist eine Geschäftsreise.

ez ist ī'-ner gesh-efts'-rī-zer.

Please don't turn everything upside down.	Bitte, bringen Sie nicht alles durcheinander.

bitt'-er, bring'-en zee nicht ull'-ez doorch'-ine-und'-er.

Have you finished?	Sind Sie fertig?

zint zee fair'-tich.

Please put a mark on them.	Bitte, machen Sie ein Zeichen darauf.

bitt'-er, maCH'-en zee ine tsī'-chen dar-owf'.

My luggage has been examined.	Mein Gepäck ist schon kontrolliert.

mine gep-eck' ist shone kon-trol-eert'.

I must hurry.	Ich muss eilen.

ich mōoss ī'-len

My train leaves in ten minutes.	Mein Zug fährt in zehn Minuten.

mine tsoog fairt in tsain min-oot'-en.

ACCOMMODATION

Furnished rooms are usually let by the week or month. The breakfast, if any, included in the price, consists only of coffee and rolls. In health resorts a municipal tax (Kurtaxe) is often added to the bill. Inquire about this point when booking rooms.

Which is the best hotel?	Welches ist das beste Hotel?

vellch'-ez ist duss best'-er ho-tell'.

Have you any rooms vacant?	Haben Sie Zimmer frei?

hah'-ben zee tsimm'-er fry.

Can you recommend another hotel?	Können Sie mir ein anderes Hotel empfehlen?

kurn'-en zee mere ine un'-der-ez ho-tell' emp-fail'-en.

I want to be in the centre of the town.	Ich möchte im Zentrum der Stadt sein.

ich murch'-er im tsent'-room dair shtutt zine.

I do not want to be in the business quarter.	Ich möchte nicht im Geschäftsviertel sein.

ich murch'-ter nicht im gesh-efts'-feer-tel zine.

I do not want to be too far out of town.	Ich möchte nicht zu weit ausserhalb der Stadt sein.

ich murcht'-er nicht tsoo vite owss'-er-hulp dair shtutt zine.

ENGAGING ROOMS

I want a single room (double room).	Ich möchte ein Einzelzimmer (Doppelzimmer.

ich murch'-er ine ine'-tsel-tsimm'-er (dopp'-el-tsimm'-er).

I want a room with two beds.	Ich möchte ein Zimmer mit zwei Betten.

ich murch'-ter ine tsimm'-er mit tsvi bet'-en.

And a bath.	Und Bad.

ŏŏnt baht.

For one night only.	Nur für eine Nacht.

noor für i'-ner naCHt.

For a week, perhaps longer.	Für eine Woche, vielleicht länger.

für i'-ner voCH'-er feel-icht' leng'-er.

We want a sitting-room as well.	Wir wollen auch ein Wohnzimmer haben.

vere voll'-en owCH ine vone'-tsimm-er hah'-ben.

Have you a lift?	Haben Sie einen Fahrstuhl?

hah'-ben zee i'-nen far'-shtool.

Let me see your rooms.	Ich möchte Ihre Zimmer ansehen.

ich murch'-ter ee'-rer tsimm'-er un'-zay-en.

| What is the price of this room (these rooms)? | Was kostet dieses Zimmer (Was kosten diese Zimmer)? |

vuss kost'-et dee'-zez tsimm'-er (vuss kost'-en dee'-zer tsimm'-er).

| That is too expensive. | Das ist zu teuer. |

duss ist tsoo toy'-er.

| Have you anything cheaper? | Haben Sie etwas Billigeres? |

hah'-ben zee et'-vuss bill'-ig-er-ez.

| That is too small. | Das ist zu klein. |

duss ist tsoo kline.

| What are your terms with full board? | Was kostet es mit voller Pension? |

vuss kost'-et ez mit foll'-er pŏñ-tsee-on'.

| How much is bed and breakfast? | Was kostet das Zimmer mit Frühstück? |

vuss kost'-et duss tsimm'-er mit frü'-shtük.

| Have you a restaurant? | Haben Sie ein Restaurant? |

hah'-ben zee ine rest'-or-ŏñ.

| I will take this room. | Ich nehme dieses Zimmer. |

ich nay'-mer dee'-zez tsimm'-er.

| What do you charge for servants' board and lodging? | Was kostet die volle Pension für Dienstboten? |

vuss kost'-et dee foll'-er pŏñ-tsee-on' für deenst'-boat-en.

| What is the number of our room? | Welche Nummer hat unser Zimmer? |

vellch'-er nŏŏm'-er hut ŏŏn'-zer tsimm'-er.

| Have our luggage sent up. | Lassen Sie unser Gepäck heraufbringen. |

luss'-en zee ŏŏn'-zer gep-eck' hair-owf'-bring-en.

Have my luggage fetched from the station.	Lassen Sie mein Gepäck vom Bahnhof holen.

luss'-en zee mine gep-eck' fom bahn'-hof hole'-en.

Can we dine in our room?	Können wir das Abendessen im Zimmer haben?

kurn'-en vere duss ah'-bent-ess-en im tsimm -er hah'-ben.

Will you have a fire lit in my room (in the sitting-room)?	Lassen Sie bitte in meinem Zimmer (im Wohnzimmer) Feuer machen?

luss'-en zee bitt'-er in mine'-em tsimm'-er (im vone'-tsimm-er) foy'-er maCH'-en.

Please open the windows wide.	Bitte machen Sie die Fenster weit auf.

bitt'-er maCH'-en zee dee fen'-ster vite owf.

Where have you put our things?	Wo haben Sie unsere Sachen hingetan?

vo hah'-ben zee ŏon'-zer-er zaCH'-en hin'-get-ahn.

Please order me the English papers.	Bitte bestellen Sie mir die englischen Zeitungen.

bitt'-er besh-tell'-en zee mere dee eng'-lich-en tsite'-ŏong-en.

Where is the bathroom, W.C.?	Wo ist das Badezimmer, die Toilette?

vo ist duss bahd'-er-tsimm-er, dee toy-lett-er.

I am going out.	Ich gehe hinaus.

ich gay'-er hin-ows'.

IN THE HOTEL

Where is the bar?	Wo ist die Bar?

vo ist dee bar.

I shall see you at dinner (in the dining-room).	Ich werde Sie beim Abendessen (im Speisesaal) wieder sehen.

ich vaird'-er zee bime ah'-bent-ess-en (im shpi'-zer-zahl) vee'-der zay'-en.

Meet me in the lounge.	Treffen Sie mich in der Diele.

treff'-en zee mich in dair dee'-ler.

| I am going to bed. | Ich gehe schlafen. |

ich gay'-er shlah'-fen.

| Please get me a bath ready. | Bitte machen Sie mir ein Bad fertig. |

bitt'-er maCH'-en zee mere ine baht fair'-tich.

| Is the room ready yet? | Ist das Zimmer schon fertig? |

ist duss tsimm'-er shone fair'-tich.

| The sheets are not properly aired. | Die Betten sind nicht gut gelüftet. |

dee bett'-en zint nicht goot gel-üft'-et.

| I should like another pillow (another blanket). | Ich möchte noch ein Kopfkissen (eine Decke) haben. |

ich murch'-ter noCH ine kopf'-kiss-en (i'-ner deck'-er) hah'-ben.

| Can you bring me a hot-water bottle? | Können Sie mir eine Wärmflasche bringen? |

kurn'-en zee mere i'-ner verm'-flush-er bring'-en.

| Will you bring me some hot water (soap, towels)? | Bringen Sie mir bitte heisses Wasser (Seife, Handtücher)? |

bring'-en zee mere bitt'-er hice'-ez vuss'-er (zī'-fer, hunt'-tüch-er).

| Please call me at —— | Bitte wecken Sie mich um—— |

bitt'-er veck'-en zee mich ōōm——

| Knock loudly. | Klopfen Sie laut. |

klopf'-en zee lout.

| Knock till I answer. | Klopfen Sie bis ich antworte. |

klopf'-en zee biss ich unt'-vort-er.

Don't disturb me in the morning.	Stören Sie mich nicht morgen früh.
	shtur'-ren zee mich nicht morg'-en frü.
Pull the curtains.	Bitte ziehen Sie den Vorhang vor.
	bitt'-er tsee'-en zee dane fore'-hung fore.
Do not close the shutters.	Machen Sie die Läden nicht zu.
	maCH'-en zee dee lay'-den nicht tsoo.
Good-night.	Gute Nacht.
	goot'-er naCHt.
Who is there?	Wer ist da?
	vair ist dah.
What time is it?	Wie spät ist es?
	vee shpate ist ez.
Wait a minute.	Warten Sie einen Augenblick.
	vart'-en zee i'-nen ow'-gen-block.
Come in!	Herein!
	hair-ine'.
Have my shoes cleaned.	Lassen Sie meine Schuhe putzen.
	luss'-en zee mi'-ner shoo'-er poot'-sen.
I want my clothes brushed (pressed).	Ich möchte meine Kleider gebürstet (gebügelt) haben.
	ich murcht'-er mi'-ner kli'-der geb-ürst'-et (geb-ü'-gelt) hah'-ben.
Please get my shoes, suit.	Bitte, bringen Sie mir meine Schuhe, meinen Anzug.
	bitt'-er bring'-en zee mere mi'-ner shoo'-er, mi'-nen un'-tsoog.

HOTEL OFFICE

Are there any letters for me ?	Sind Briefe für mich angekommen ?

zint brief'-er für mich un'-gek-omm-en.

Has anyone asked for me ?	Hat jemand nach mir gefragt ?

hut yay'-munt naCH mere gef-rahgt'.

Did anyone ring up for me ?	Hat jemand für mich angerufen ?

hut yay'-munt für mich un'-ger-oof-en.

I want to post a letter.	Ich möchte einen Brief aufgeben.

ich murcht'-er ī'-nen brief owf'-gay-ben.

Is —— still in his (her) room ?	Ist —— noch in seinem (ihrem) Zimmer ?

ist——noCH in zī'-nem (ee'-rem) tsimm'-er.

What is the number of his (her) room ?	Welche Nummer hat sein (ihr) Zimmer ?

vellch'-er nŏŏm'-er hut zine (eer) tsimm'-er.

Will you send up a messenger ?	Bitte schicken Sie einen Boten hinauf ?

bitt'-er shick'-en zee ī'-nen boat'-en hin-owf'.

I want some theatre tickets.	Ich möchte Theaterkarten haben.

ich murcht'-er tay-aht'-er-kart-en hah'-ben.

What is the best play, revue, musical comedy ?	Was ist das beste Stück, die beste Revue, Operette ?

vuss ist duss best'-er shtük, dee best'-er rev-ü, o-per-ett'-er.

Is the opera on ?	Gibt es eine Oper ?

geebt ez ī'-ner ō'-per.

What time does it begin ?	Wann fängt es an ?

vunn fengt ez un.

| Ought I to dress ? | Muss ich Abendanzug tragen ? |

mŏŏss *ich* ah'-bent-un'-tsoog trah'-gen.

| Is it easy to get tickets ? | Bekommt man leicht Karten ? |

bek-ommt' mun lĭcht kart'-en.

| Will you try for me ? | Wollen Sie es für mich versuchen ? |

voll'-en zee ez für mi*ch* fair-sooCH'-en.

| Is there a night porter on duty ? | Ist ein Nachtportier hier ? |

ist ine naCHt'-port-yay here.

| Shall I be able to get anything to eat on my return ? | Werde ich etwas zu essen bekommen, wenn ich zurück-komme ? |

vair'-de*r* *ich* et'-vuss tsoo ess'-en bek-omm'-en, venn i*ch* tsoo-rük'-komm-e*r*.

| I want to see the manager. | Ich möchte den Direk-tor sprechen. |

ich mu*rch*t'-e*r* dane dee-rect'-or shpre*ch*'-en.

LEAVING THE HOTEL

| Get my bill ready, please. | Bitte machen Sie meine Rechnung fertig. |

bitt'-e*r* maCH'-en zee mī-ne*r* re*ch*'-nŏŏng fair'-ti*ch*.

| Will you take a travellers' cheque ? | Nehmen Sie einen Reisescheck ? |

nay'-men zee ī'-nen rī'-zer-sheck.

| How much does the bill come to ? | Wieviel macht die Rechnung ? |

vee-feel' maCHt dee re*ch*'-nŏŏng.

| What are these charges for ? | Wofür sind diese Beträge ? |

vo-für' zint dee'-ze*r* bet-ray'-ge*r*.

I think you have made a mistake.	Ich glaube, Sie haben sich geirrt.
ich glow'-ber, zee hah'-ben s*ich* ge-irrt'.	
We did not have———	Wir haben kein ——— gehabt.
vere hah'-ben kine—ge-hupt'.	
You said the rooms only cost———	Sie sagten, die Zimmer kosten nur———
zee zaCHt'-en, dee tsimm'-er kost'-en noor———	
Please give me a receipt.	Bitte geben Sie mir eine Quittung.
bitt'-er gay'-ben zee mere ī'-ner k-vitt'-ŏong.	
Give me some small change.	Geben Sie mir etwas Kleingeld.
gay'-ben zee mere et'-vuss kline'-gelt.	
Do I tip, or is there a charge for service ?	Muss ich Trinkgeld geben, oder wird die Bedienung berechnet ?
mŏoss i*ch* trink'-gelt gay'-ben, ŏ'-der virt dee bed-een'-ŏong ber-e*ch*'-net.	
Divide that between you.	Verteilen Sie das unter einander.
Fair-tile'-en zee duss ŏon'-ter-i-nun-dare.	
I am leaving to-night.	Ich reise heute abend ab.
ich rī'-zer hoy'-ter ah'bent up.	
Have my luggage brought down.	Lassen Sie mein Gepäck herunterbringen.
luss'-en zee mine gep-eck' hair-ŏon'-ter-bring-en.	
Send my luggage to the station.	Schicken Sie mein Gepäck zum Bahnhof.
shick'-en zee mīne gep-eck' tsŏom bahn'-hofe.	
When does the hotel bus go ?	Wann fährt der Hotel⁻wagen ?
vunn fairt dair ho-tell'-vah-gen.	

How soon ought I to leave ?	Wann muss ich hier fortgehen ?
	vunn mŏŏss ich here fort'-gay-en.

How long does it take to the station ?	Wie lange brauche ich zum Bahnhof ?
	vee lung'-er browCH'-er ich tsŏŏm bahn'-hofe.

Can I walk ?	Kann ich laufen ?
	kun ich low'-fen.

I have been very comfortable.	Ich habe mich sehr wohl gefühlt.
	ich hah'-ber mich zair vole gef-ült'.

If any letters come for me, please forward them to——	Wenn noch Briefe für mich ankommen, senden Sie sie bitte nach an——
	venn noCH brief'-er für mich un'-komm-en, zend'-en zee zee bitt'-er naCH un——

Have you any labels ?	Haben Sie Etiketten ?
	hah'-ben zee et-i-kett'-en.

Have some sandwiches packed for me to take on the journey.	Lassen Sie mir ein paar belegte Brote für die Reise einpacken.
	luss'-en zee mere ine par bel-aygt'-er brŏ'-ter für dee rī'-zer ine'-puck-en.

I am not going till the night train.	Ich fahre erst mit dem Nachtzug.
	ich far'-er airst mit dame naCHt'-tsoog.

When must I leave my room ?	Wann muss ich mein Zimmer verlassen ?
	vunn mŏŏss ich mine tsimm'-er fair-luss'-en.

Can I leave my luggage here ?	Kann ich mein Gepäck hier lassen ?
	kunn ich mine gep-eck' here luss'-en.

Can you let me have a room to change in this evening ?	Können Sie mir ein Zimmer geben, wo ich mich heute abend umziehen kann ?

kurn'-en zee mere ine tsimm'-er gay-ben, vo ich mich
hoy'-ter ah'-bent ŏŏm'-tsee-en kun.

LAUNDRY

For washing list see vocabulary under " Shopping."

I have some things for the laundry.	Ich will etwas in die Wäscherei schicken.

ich vill et'-vuss in dee vesh'-eri shick'-en.

When does it go ?	Wann wird es abgeholt ?

vunn virt ez up'-ge-hōlt.

When is it returned ?	Wann kommt es zurück ?

vunn kommt ez tsoo-rük.

Can I have these things back in two days ?	Kann ich diese Sachen in zwei Tagen wieder haben ?

kunn ich dee'-zer saCH'-en in tsvī tahg'-en vee'-der hah'-ben.

I am leaving on Thursday.	Ich reise Donnerstag ab.

ich rī'-zer donn'-ers-tahg up.

Let me have the shirts and collars back as soon as possible ; I am not in such a hurry for the rest.	Die Hemden und Kragen brauche ich so bald wie möglich ; das Übrige eilt nicht so sehr.

dee hemt'-en ŏŏnt krah'-gen browCH'-er ich zo bult vee
murg'-lich ; duss ü'-brig-er īlt nicht zo zair.

These collars are not to be starched.	Diese Kragen sollen nicht gestärkt werden.

dee'-zer krah'-gen zoll'-en nicht ge-shtairkt' vair'-den.

There are two handkerchiefs missing.	Es fehlen zwei Taschentücher.

ez fail'-en tsvī tush'-en-tüch-er.

Some of the things want mending.	Einige Sachen müssen gestopft werden.

ī′-nig-e*r* saCH′-en müss′-en gesh-topft′ vair′-den.

Can you have them mended in the hotel for me ?	Können Sie sie im Hotel stopfen lassen ?

ku*r*n′-en zee zee im ho-tel′ shtopf′-en luss′-en.

Can you send my laundry on to this address if it is not back in time ?	Können Sie meine Wäsche an diese Adresse nachschicken, wenn sie nicht zur rechten Zeit zurück- kommt ?

ku*r*n′-en zee mī′-ne*r* vesh′-e*r* un dee′-ze*r* a-dress′-e*r* naCH′- shick-en venn zee ni*ch*t tsoor re*ch*t′-en tsite tsoo-rük′-kommt.

LOCAL TRAVELLING, EXCURSIONS

FINDING THE WAY

Where can I get a guide- book, a map of the town ?	Wo kann ich einen Führ- er (eine Karte) von der Stadt bekommen ?

vo kun i*ch* ī′-nen für′-er (ī′-ne*r* kart′-e*r*) fon dair shtutt bek-omm′-en.

It must be in English.	Es muss in englischer Sprache sein.

ez mŏŏss in eng′-lish-er shpraCH′-e*r* zine.

Would you be so good as to direct me to——?	Würden Sie so gut sein, mir den Weg nach —— zu zeigen ?

vürd′-en zee zo goot zine, me*r*e dane vaig naCH—tsoo tsī′-gen.

Is this the right way to——?	Komme ich auf diesem Weg nach——?

komm′-e*r* i*ch* owf dee′-zem vaig naCH——

Is this the shortest way to——?	Ist dies der kürzeste Weg nach——?

ist deess dair kürts'-est-er vaig naCH——

How long does it take ?	Wie lange dauert es ?

vee lung'-er dow'-ert ez.

Can I walk or must I take a taxi ?	Kann ich zu Fuss gehen, oder muss ich einen Wagen nehmen ?

kun ich tsoo fooss gay'-en, o'-der mooss ich ī'-nen vah'-gen nay'-men.

Can I go by bus, tram, underground ?	Kann ich mit dem Autobus (mit der Strassenbahn, mit der Untergrundbahn) fahren ?

kun ich mit dame ow'-to-booss (mit dare shtrahss'-en-bahn, mit dare oon'-ter-groont-bahn far'-en.

Where is the nearest bus stop, tram stop ?	Wo ist die nächste Haltestelle ?

vo ist dee next'-er hult'-er-shtell-er.

Where is the tube station ?	Wo ist der Untergrundbahnhof ?

vo ist dare oon'-ter-groont-bahn-hofe.

Does this tram go to the Opera House, to the General Post Office, to the Central Station?	Fährt diese Bahn zum Opernhaus (zur Hauptpost, zum Hauptbahnhof) ?

fairt dee'-zer bahn tsoom ō'-pern-house (tsoor howpt'-posst, tsoom howpt'-bahn-hofe).

Is that the terminus ?	Ist das die Endhaltestelle ?

ist duss dee ent'-hult-er-shtell-er.

Do I have to change ?	Muss ich umsteigen ?

mooss ich oom'-shtī-gen.

Does the electric train go there ?	Fährt der elektrische Zug dahin ?

fairt dare el-ek'-trish-er tsoog dah-hin'.

Can one drive right up to the top ?	Kann man den ganzen Weg im Auto hinauf fahren ?

kun mun dane gunts'-en vaig im ow'-to hin-owf' far'-en.

Straight ahead ?	Gerade aus ?

ge*r*-rah'-de*r* owce.

To the right, left ?	Rechts, links ?

re*ch*ts, links.

First on the right.	Die erste rechts.

dee airst'-e*r* re*ch*ts.

Second on the left.	Die zweite links.

dee tsvī'-te*r* links.

Keep straight on.	Immer gerade aus.

imm'-er ge*r*-rah'-de*r* owce.

I might miss the way.	Ich könnte den Weg verfehlen.

ich ku*r*n'-te*r* dane vaig fair-fail'-en.

I prefer to take a taxi.	Ich nehme lieber einen Wagen.

ich nay'-me*r* lee'-ber i'-nen vah'-gen.

Please drive to——	Bitte fahren Sie nach——

bitt'-er far'-en zee naCH——

GOING BY TRAIN

Where is the booking-office ?	Wo ist der Fahrkarten-schalter ?

vo ist dare far'-kart-en-shult-er.

What station must I ask for ?	Nach welchem Bahnhof muss ich fragen ?

naCH vell*ch*'-em bahn'-hofe mööss *ich* frah'-gen.

Which platform ?	Welcher Bahnsteig ?

vell*ch*'-er bahn'-shtīg.

Should I take the next train ?	Soll ich den nächsten Zug nehmen ?

zoll *ich* dane next'-en tsoog nay'-men.

G.   C

Is this the right train for——?	Ist dies der richtige Zug nach——?

ist deess dare richt'-ig-er tsoog nuCH—

Where do I get out ?	Wo muss ich aussteigen?

vo mōōss ich ows'-shtī-gen.

Does this train stop at——?	Hält dieser Zug in——?

helt dee'-zer tsoog in——

Must I change ?	Muss ich umsteigen ?

mōōss ich ōōm'-shtī-gen.

Where must I change ?	Wo muss ich umsteigen ?

vo mōōss ich ōōm'-shtī-gen.

I can't open the door.	Ich kann die Tür nicht aufmachen.

ich kun dee tür nicht owf'-maCH-en.

Can you tell me, am I in the right train for——?	Können Sie mir sagen, ob ich im richtigen Zug nach—— bin ?

kurn'-en zee mere zah'-gen, op ich im richt'-ig-en tsoog nuCH—bin.

GOING BY MOTOR

I want to hire a car.	Ich möchte ein Auto mieten.

ich murcht'-er ine ow'-to mee'-ten.

Have you a driver who speaks English ?	Haben Sie einen Chauffeur, der englisch spricht ?

hah'-ben zee ī'-nen sho-fur' dare eng'-lish shpricht.

How much do you charge per day, per kilometer ?	Wieviel verlangen Sie pro Tag, pro Kilometer ?

vee-feel' fair-lung'-en zee pro tahg, pro keel'-o-mait-er.

How much do you want for the whole trip ?	Wieviel verlangen Sie für die ganze Fahrt ?

vee-feel' fair-lung'-en zee für dee gunts'-er fahrt.

Tip included.	einschliesslich Trinkgeld.

ine'-shleess-lich trink'-gelt.

How many miles is it ? (1 mile = 1.6 kilometer)	Wieviel Kilometer sind es ?

vee-feel' keel'-o-mait-er zint ez.

How long will it take ?	Wie lange wird es dauern ?

vee lung'-er virt ez dow'-ern.

SIGHT-SEEING

I want an English-speaking guide.	Ich möchte einen Führer, der Englisch spricht.

ich murcht'-er ï'-nen für'-er dare eng'-lish shpricht.

I want to see all that is worth seeing.	Ich möchte alles sehen, was sehenswert ist.

ich murcht'-er ull'-es zay'-en vuss zay'-ens-vairt ist.

I have very little time.	Ich habe sehr wenig Zeit.

ich hah'-ber zair vay'-nich tsite.

Have we time to see——?	Haben wir Zeit, —— zu sehen ?

hah'-ben vere tsite—tsoo zay'-en.

What street, church, building is that ?	Was ist das für eine Strasse, Kirche, für ein Gebäude ?

vuss ist duss für ï'-ner strahss'-er, keerch'-er, für ine geb-oy'-der.

I am interested in picture galleries.	Ich interessiere mich für Gemälde-Galerien.

ich in-ter-ess-eer'-er mich für ge-meld'-er-gal-er-ee-en.

I shall not have time for museums.	Ich werde keine Zeit für Museen haben.

ich vair'-der kï'-ner tsite für moo-zay'-en hah'-ben.

I must see the cathedral.	Ich muss den Dom sehen.

ich mŏŏss dane dome zay'-en.

I want to see the town hall, the university first.	Ich möchte zuerst das Rathaus, die Universität sehen.

ich murcht'-er tsoo-airst' duss raht'-house, dee ŏŏn-ee-fair-zee-tate' zay'-en.

Drive back through the park.	Fahren Sie durch den Park zurück.

far'-en zee dŏŏrch dane park tsoo-rük.

I should like to see the botanical (zoological) gardens now.	Ich möchte jetzt den botanischen (zoologischen) Garten sehen.

ich murcht'-er yetst dane bot-ahn'-ish-en (tso-lo'-gish-en) gart'-en zay'-en.

Please wait for me here.	Bitte warten Sie hier auf mich.

bitt'-er vart'-en zee here owf mich.

What is that?	Was ist das?

vuss ist duss.

Is it worth getting out?	Lohnt es sich, auszusteigen?

loant ez zich, owce'-tsoo-shtī-gen.

Is it still open?	Ist es noch offen?

ist ez noCH off'-en.

How long does —— stay open?	Wie lange bleibt —— offen?

vee lung'-er blībt—off'-en.

On what days (when) is —— open to the public?	An welchen Tagen (wann) ist —— für das Publikum geöffnet?

un vellch'-en tahg'-en (vun) ist—für duss poob'-lick-ŏŏm ge-urf'-net.

Can one see over the castle ?	Kann man das Schloss besichtigen ?

kun mun duss shloss bez-*ich*t'-ig-en.

To whom must I apply for admission ?	Wen kann ich um Ein-lass bitten ?

vane kun i*ch* õõm ine'-luss bitt'-en.

Can we go round alone, or do we have to take a guide ?	Dürfen wir allein her-umgehen, oder müssen wir einen Führer haben ?

dür'-fen vere ul-ine' hair-õõm'-gay-en, o'-der müss'-en vere i'-nen für'-er hah'-ben.

How long must we wait ?	Wie lange müssen wir warten ?

vee lung'-er müss'-en vere var'-ten.

When does the next tour start ?	Wann beginnt die nächste Führung ?

vunn beg-innt' dee next'-er für'-õõng.

How long does the tour take ?	Wie lange dauert die Führung ?

vee lung'-er dow'-ert dee für'-õõng.

Where are the picture-galleries ?	Wo sind die Gemälde-galerien ?

vo zint dee ge-meld'-er-gal-er-ee-en.

Where is the sculpture ?	Wo sind die Skulpturen?

vo zint dee Shkõõlp toor'-en.

I do not care for that.	Das gefällt mir nicht.

duss gef-ellt' mere ni*ch*t.

How much farther does this go ?	Wie weit geht es noch ?

vee vite gait ez noCH.

How many more rooms are there ?	Wie viele Zimmer gibt es noch ?

vee feel'-er tsimm'-er geebt ez noCH.

How many steps are there ?	Wie viele Stufen sind es ?

vee feel'-er stoof'-en zint ez.

Is there a good view ?	Hat man eine schöne Aussicht ?

hut mun ī'-ner shurn'-er owce'-zicht.

May I photograph here ?	Darf ich hier photographieren ?

darf ich here photo-graph-eer'-en.

Please stop here a moment, I want to take a photograph.	Bitte halten Sie hier einen Augenblick, ich will eine Aufnahme machen.

bitt'-er hult'-en zee here ī'-nen owg'-en-blick, ich vill ī'-ner
owf'-nahm-er maCH'-en.

Is that the —— Memorial ?	Ist das das —— Denkmal ?

ist duss duss—denk'-mahl.

Where is —— buried ?	Wo ist —— begraben ?

vo ist—beg-rahb'-en.

Did —— live in this house ?	Hat —— in diesem Haus gewohnt ?

hut—in dee'-zem house gev-ōnt'.

What is the name of that mountain, lake, river ?	Wie heisst der Berg, See, Strom ?

vee hīsst dair bairg, zay, shtroam.

Is there a funicular railway ?	Gibt es eine Seilbahn ?

geebt ez ī'-ner zile'-bahn.

Does one have to walk ?	Muss man zu Fuss gehen ?

mōōss mun tsoo fooss gay'-en.

Is it very far ?	Ist es sehr weit ?

ist ez zair vite.

Is there a restaurant at the top ?	Gibt es ein Restaurant auf dem Berge ?

geebt ez ine rest-o-rang' owf dame berg'-er.

Let us go up then.	Dann wollen wir hinauf-gehen.

dun voll'-en vere hin-owf'-gay-en.

Let us go for a walk along the lakeside.	Gehen wir am See ent-lang spazieren.

gay'-en vere am zay ent-lung' shputs-eer'-en.

Can I get any pictures ?	Kann ich Bilder bekom-men ?

kun ich bild'-er bek-omm'-en.

How much is the cata-logue ?	Was kostet der Kata-log ?

vuss kost'-et dair kut-ul-ōg'.

Have you a book about——?	Haben Sie ein Buch über——?

hah'-ben zee ine booCH ü'-ber——

I want to write some post-cards.	Ich möchte Ansichts-karten schreiben.

ich murch'-ter un'-zichts-kart-en shrī'-ben.

Where can we get some-thing to eat, drink ?	Wo können wir etwas zu essen (trinken), bek-ommen ?

vo kurn'-en vere et'-vuss tsoo ess'-en (trink'-en) bek-omm'-en.

I am too tired to go any further.	Ich bin zu müde, um weiter zu gehen.

ich bin tsoo mü'-der ŏŏm vī'-ter tsoo gay'-en.

It is too hot ; I have seen enough for to-day.	Es ist zu warm ; ich habe für heute genug gesehen.

ez ist tsoo varm ; ich hah'-ber für hoy'-ter gen-ooCH' gez-ay'-en.

It is going to rain.	Es wird regnen.

ez virt raig'-nen.

We ought to turn back.	Wir sollten umkehren.
	vere zol'-ten ōōm'-kair-en.
Lend me your umbrella.	Leihen Sie mir Ihren Schirm.
	lī'-en zee mere ee'-ren sheerm.
Let us take shelter here.	Wir wollen uns hier unterstellen.
	vere voll'-en ōōns here ōōn'-ter-shtell-en.
Can we get a taxi?	Können wir einen Taxi bekommen?
	kurn'-en vere ī'-nen tucks'-ee bek-omm'-en.
Which is the best way back?	Was ist der beste Weg zurück?
	vuss ist dair best'-er vaig tsoo-rük'.
Drive to the —— Hotel as quickly as possible.	Fahren Sie so schnell wie möglich zum Hotel——
	far'-en zee zo shnell vee murg'-lich tsōōm ho-tell'——
Drive back by way of——	Fahren Sie über —— zurück.
	far'-en zee ü'-ber—tsoo-rük'.
How much ought I to give the guide?	Wieviel muss ich dem Führer geben?
	vee-feel mōōss ich dame fü'-rer gay'-ben.
Thank you very much.	Danke sehr.
	dunk'-er zair.
Are you free to-morrow?	Sind Sie morgen frei?
	zint zee mor'-gen fry.
Please be at the hotel to-morrow morning at 10.	Bitte kommen Sie morgen früh um zehn Uhr zum Hotel.
	bitt'-er komm'-en zee mor'-gen frü ōōm tsain oor tsōōm ho-tell'
We are leaving the day after to-morrow.	Wir fahren übermorgen ab.
	vere far'-en ü'-ber-mor-gen up.

VISITING FRIENDS

Is this where —— lives ? võnt here.	Wohnt hier——?
Is he (she) at home ? ist air (zee) tsoo how'-zer.	Ist er (sie) zu Hause ?
It is Mr. (Mrs., Miss)—— mine nah'-mer ist——	Mein Name ist —— (without prefix).
Here is my card. here ist mī'-ner kart'-er.	Hier ist meine Karte.
May I introduce myself ; I am—— darf ich mich fore'-shtell-en ; mine nah'-mer ist——	Darf ich mich vorstellen; mein Name ist——
Let me introduce my wife, daughter, son, husband, uncle, nephew, aunt, niece. gesh-tutt'-en zee, duss ich fore'-shtell-er, mī'-ner frow, toCH'-ter, mine zone, mun, onk'-el, neff'-er, mī'-ner tun'-ter, nicht'-er.	Gestatten Sie, dass ich vorstelle : meine Frau, Tochter, mein Sohn, Mann, Onkel, Neffe, meine Tante, Nichte.
Delighted to meet you. zair un'-gen-aim.	Sehr angenehm.
How do you do ? vee gate ez ee'-nen.	Wie geht es Ihnen ?
I have a letter for you from—— ich hah'-ber ī'-nen brief un zee fon——	Ich habe einen Brief an Sie von——
I have a letter of recommendation from Professor—— ich hah'-ber ī'-nen emp-fail'-ōongs-brief fon hairn pro-fess'-or——	Ich habe einen Empfehlungsbrief von Herrn Professor——

He is a great friend of mine.	Er ist ein guter Freund von mir.

air ist ine goot'-er froynt fon mere.

I have known him a long time.	Ich kenne ihn seit langem.

ich kenn'-er een zite lung'-em.

I got to know him in——	Ich habe ihn in —— kennen gelernt.

ich hah'-ber een in—kenn'-en gel-airnt.

Mr. —— asked me to look you up.	Herr —— bat mich, Sie aufzusuchen.

hair—baht mich, zee owf'-tsoo-zooCH-en.

He sends you his kindest regards, his love.	Er lässt Sie bestens grüssen, herzlich grüssen.

air lesst zee best'-enz grüss'-en, hairts'-lich grüss'-en.

I speak very little German.	Ich spreche sehr schlecht deutsch.

ich shprech'-er zair shlecht doytsh.

I should like to very much.	Sehr gern.

zair gairn

When shall I be ready?	Wann soll ich fertig sein?

vunn zoll ich fair'-tich zine.

When shall we be back?	Wann werden wir zurück sein?

vunn vair'-den vere tsoo-rük' zine.

Will you call for me at my hotel?	Wollen Sie mich in meinem Hotel abholen?

voll'-en zee mich in mī'-nem ho-tell' up'-hole-en.

What should I wear?	Was soll ich anziehen?

vuss zoll ich un'-tsee-en.

When shall we meet?	Wann sollen wir uns treffen?

vunn zoll'-en vere ŏŏns treff'-en.

| When shall I see you again ? | Wann werde ich Sie wieder sehen ? |

vunn vair'-der ich zee vee'-der zay'-en.

| Please do not bother to come to the door. | Bitte bemühen Sie sich nicht zur Tür. |

bitt'-er bem-ü'-en zee zich nicht tsoor tür.

| Thank you very much. | Ich danke Ihnen vielmals. |

ich dunk'-er ee'-nen feel'-mulce.

| I am so glad to have met you. | Ich freue mich, Sie kennen gelernt zu haben. |

ich froy'-er mich, zee kenn'-en gel-airnt tsoo hah'-ben.

| The pleasure is mine. | Ganz meinerseits. |

gunts mī'-ner-zites.

| Are you likely ever to be coming to England ? | Kommen Sie vielleicht einmal nach England ? |

komm'-en zee feel-licht ine-mahl naCH eng'-lunt.

| Please take my address and let me know if you are coming to—— | Bitte notieren Sie meine Adresse, und schreiben Sie mir, wenn Sie nach —— kommen. |

bitt'-er no-teer'-en zee mī'-ner a-dress'-er, ŏont shrī'-ben zee mere, venn zee naCH—komm'-en.

| Good-bye ; I shall tell —— that I have seen you and found you well. | Auf Wiedersehen ; ich werde ——sagen, dass ich Sie gesehen und gesund angetroffen habe. |

owf vee'-der-zay-en ; ich vair'-der—zah'-gen, duss ich zee gez-ay'-en ŏont gez-ŏont un'-get-roff-en hah'-ber.

SHOPPING

In many German cities the main shopping centre suffered extensive bomb damage. Almost all the shops, however, have managed to carry on their business, and new premises are being built and old ones repaired fairly rapidly. As in Britain, there are some large department stores which sell all kinds of goods. These are generally held to be cheaper than, though not so good as, the smaller specialised shops. Service is usually efficient, and in most shops one can find an assistant with some knowledge of English. In Switzerland, English is even more widely understood in shops, especially in the cities and tourist centres. In both countries, sizes are marked differently from the British system, though this will often be understood. Clothing is measured in centimetres (1 inch is rather less than 2½ centimetres), and cloth is sold by the metre (1 metre is just under 40 inches). A German pound is roughly 10 per cent more than the British pound; a kilogram equals two German pounds.

THE TOBACCONIST

Where is the tobacconist ? | Wo ist ein Zigarren-geschäft ?

vo ist ine tsee-gar'-en-gesh-eft.

I want some tobacco. | Ich möchte etwas Tabak.

ich mu*r*ch'-te*r* et'-vuss tah-buk'

Have you British, American, Turkish cigarettes ? | Haben Sie englische, amerikanische, türkische Zigaretten ?

hah'-ben zee eng'-lish-e*r*, um-air-ik-ahn'-ish-e*r*, türk'-ish-e*r* tsi-gar-ett'-en.

How much are these ? | Was kosten diese ?

vuss kost'-en dee'-ze*r*.

Have you anything cheaper ? | Haben Sie etwas Billigeres ?

hah'-ben zee et'-vuss bill'-ig-er-ez.

I'll take these. | Ich nehme diese.

ich nay'-mer dee'-ze*r*.

| I want some matches. | Ich möchte Streichhöl-zer haben. |
| | *ich murch'-ter shtrīch'-hurl-tser hah'-ben.* |

| I want some cheap cigars. | Ich hätte gern eine billige Zigarre |
| | *ich hett'-er gairn ī'-ner bill'-ig-er tsi-gar'-er.* |

| Give me a box of ten, twenty-five, fifty. | Geben Sie mir eine Schachtel (if wood, " Kiste ") mit zehn, fünfundzwanzig, fünf-zig. |
| | *gay'-ben zee mere ī'-ner shaCH'-tel (kiss'-ter) mit tsain, fünf-ōōnt-tsvunt'-sich, fünf'-tsich.* |

| Can you change a hun-dred-Mark note ? | Können Sie hundert-Mark wechseln ? |
| | *kurn'-en zee hōōnd'-ert mark vex'-eln.* |

| How late do you remain open ? | Wie lange haben Sie offen ? |
| | *vee lung'-er hah'-ben zee off'-en.* |

| Are you open on Sun-days ? | Öffnen Sie sonntags ? |
| | *urf'-nen zee zonn'-tahgs.* |

| Cigar-, cigarette-case. | Zigarren- (Zigaretten-) etui. |
| | *tsi-gar'-en- (tsi-gar-ett'-en)-ay-twee'.* |

| Cigar- (cigarette-) holder. | Zigarren- (Zigaretten-) spitze. |
| | *tsi-gar'-en-(tsi-gar-ett'-en-) shpits'-er.* |

| Pipe, pipe-cleaner. | Pfeife, Pfeifenreiniger. |
| | *pfī'-fer, pfī'-fen-rī'-nig-er.* |

| Lighter, Fuel. | Feuerzeug, Brennstoff. |
| | *foy'-er-tsoyg, brenn'-shtoff.* |

| Flint, wick. | Feuerstein, Docht. |
| | *foy'-er-shtine, doCHt.* |

THE POST OFFICE

In the larger offices an official can usually be found who under-
stands some English. Passports may be required for some services.
In Germany and Switzerland letter-boxes are painted yellow
and are frequently built flush with a wall, making them difficult
to find at first. In Switzerland, Air-mail letters should be handed
in at a post office ; if put in a letter-box they will be sent by
ordinary mail.

Which is the way to the G.P.O., to the Post Office ?	Wie komme ich zur Hauptpost (zum Post-amt) ?

vee komm´-er *ich* tsoor howpt´-posst (tsŏŏm posst´-umt).

I want stamps.	Ich möchte Briefmarken.

ich mu*rch*t´-e*r* brief´-mark-en.

How much are letters for abroad ? and post-cards ?	Was kosten Briefe ins Ausland ? und Post-karten ?

vuss kost´-en brief´-er inz owce´-lunt ? ŏŏnt posst´-kart-en;

Will this go to-night ?	Geht das heute abend fort ?

gate duss hoy´-te*r* ah´-bent fort.

This is to go air-mail.	Das soll mit Flugpost gehen.

duss zoll mit floog´-posst gay´-en.

I want to register this letter, parcel.	Ich möchte diesen Brief (dieses Paket) ein-schreiben lassen.

i*ch* mu*rch*t´-e*r* dee´-zen brief (dee´-zez puck-ate´) ine´-shrī-ben luss´-en.

Which window do I go to ?	Zu welchem Schalter muss ich gehen ?

tsoo vell*ch*´-em shult´-er mŏŏss *ich* gay´-en.

Will this go letter post ?	Geht das als Brief ?

gate duss ulce brief.

I want to send this parcel.	Ich möchte dieses Paket aufgeben.

i*ch* mu*rch*t´-e*r* dee´-zez puck-ate´ owf´-gay-ben.

| I have left the ends open; there are only books inside. | Ich habe die Enden offen gelassen; es sind nur Bücher drin. |

ich hah'-ber dee end'-en off'-en gel-uss'-en; ez zint noor büch'-er drin.

| This parcel is fragile, please be careful. | Dieses Paket ist zerbrechlich, bitte seien Sie vorsichtig. |

dee'-zez puck-ate' ist tsair-brech'-lich, bitt'-er zī'-en zee fore'-zicht-*ich*.

| These goods are perishable. | Es sind verderbliche Waren. |

ez zint fair-derb'-lich-er-var'-en.

| I want to send a telegram. | Ich möchte ein Telegramm aufgeben. |

ich murch'-ter ine tel-ay-grumm' owf'-gay-ben.

| Where are telegraph forms? | Wo sind die Telegramm-Formulare? |

vo zint dee tel-ay-grumm'-form-oo-lar'-er.

| This is for abroad. | Dies ist fürs Ausland. |

deess ist fürz owce'-lunt.

| There is nothing dutiable in this package. | Es ist nichts Verzollbares in diesem Paket. |

ez ist nichts fair-tsoll'-bar-ez in dee'-zem puck-ate'.

| Where do I cash money orders? | Wo bekommt man Post-Anweisungen ausgezahlt? |

vo bek-ommt' mun posst'-un-vī-zōōng-en owce'-get-sahlt.

| Where is the Poste Restante? | Wo sind postlagernde Briefe? |

vo zint posst'-lahg'-ern-der brief'-er.

| Are there any letters for me in the Poste Restante | Sind postlagernde Briefe für mich da? |

zint posst'-lahg'-ern-der brief'-er für mich dah.

I spell my name——	Mein Name schreibt sich——

mine nahm'-er shrībt zich——

THE CHEMIST

Can you recommend me a good chemist where they speak English?	Können Sie mir eine gute Apotheke empfehlen, wo man englisch spricht?

kurn'-en zee mere i'-ner goot'-er up-o-tay'-ker emp-fay'-len, vo mun eng'-lish shpricht.

Can you make up an English prescription?	Können Sie ein englisches Rezept herstellen?

kurn'-en zee ine eng'-lish-ez ray-tsept' hair'-shtell-en.

Please make up this prescription.	Bitte machen Sie dieses Rezept.

bitt'-er maCH'-en zee dee'-zez ray-tsept'.

I shall call for it later.	Ich werde es später abholen.

ich vair'-der ez shpate'-er up'-ho-len.

Can you give me something for constipation, diarrhoea, hay fever?	Können Sie mir etwas geben für Verstopfung, Durchfall, Heufieber?

kurn'-en zee mere et'-vuss gay'-ben für fair-shtopf'-ŏong doorch'-fal, hoy'-fee-ber.

Can one drink the water here?	Kann man das Wasser hier trinken?

kun mun duss vuss'-er here trink'-en.

I have a bad cold in my head, on my chest.	Ich habe einen schweren Schnupfen, eine schwere Brusterkältung.

ich hah'-ber i'-nen shvair'-en shnŏop'-fen, i'-ner shvair'-er broost'-air-kelt-ŏong.

| I feel faint, giddy. | Ich fühle mich schwach, schwindlig. |

ich fül'-er mich shvaCH, shvhvind'-lich.

| I feel sick, feverish. | Ich fühle mich schlecht, fiebrig. |

ich fül'-er mich shlecht, feeb'-rich.

| I am overtired. | Ich bin übermüdet. |

ich bin ü'-ber-müd-et.

| I have a headache, stomach-ache. | Ich habe Kopfschmerzen, Magenschmerzen |

ich hah'-ber kopf'-shmair-tsen, mah'-gen-shmair-tsen.

| I have earache, tooth-ache. | Ich habe Ohrenschmerzen, Zahnschmerzen. |

ich hah'-ber o'-ren-shmair-tsen, tsahn'-shmair-tsen.

| My feet are sore. | Die Füsse tun mir weh. |

dee füss'-er toon mere vay.

| I have blisters, corns. | Ich habe Blasen, Hühneraugen. |

ich hah'-ber blah'-zen, hü'-ner-owg-en.

| I have some mosquito bites ; give me some ammonia. | Ich habe Moskitostiche ; geben Sie mir etwas Ammoniak. |

ich hah'-ber mos-kee'-to-shtich'-er ; gay'-ben zee mere et'-vuss um-on-ee-ack'.

| My hands are chapped. | Die Hände sind mir aufgesprungen. |

dee hend'-er zint mere owf'-gesh-proong-en.

| My back is badly sun-burnt. | Ich habe Sonnenbrand im Rücken. |

ich hah'-ber zonn'-en-brunt im rük'-en.

| Can you give me something to rub on it ? | Können Sie mir etwas zum Einreiben geben ? |

kurn'-en zee mere et'-vuss tsoom ine'-rī-ben gay'-ben.

| Have you fruit-salts ? | Haben Sie Fruchtsalz ? |

hah'-ben zee frooCHt'-zults.

| May I speak to a male, female attendant ? | Darf ich Herrenbedienung, Damenbedienung haben ? |

darf *ich* hair'-en-bed-een-ŏong, dahm'-en-bed-een-ŏong hah'-ben.

| Can you recommend a doctor, surgeon ? | Können Sie mir einen Arzt, Chirurgen empfehlen ? |

ku*r*n'-en zee mere ī'-nen artst, *ch*ir-ŏŏr'-gen emp-fay'-len.

| I should like to see a specialist in—— | Ich möchte einen Spezialisten für —— sehen. |

ich mu*r*cht'-e*r* ī'-nen shpait-si-al-ist'-en für—zay'-en.

| Is there a hospital, nursing-home ? | Gibt es ein Krankenhaus, eine Klinik ? |

geebt ez ine krunk'-en-house, ī'-ne*r* kleen'-eek.

| Aperient, Bandage. | Abführmittel, Verband. |

up'-für-mitt-el, fair-bunt'.

| Crepe bandage, Bath salts. | Kreppverband, Badesalz. |

krepp'-fair-bunt, bahd'-e*r*-zults.

| Castor oil, Comb. | Rizinusöl, Kamm. |

ree'-tsin-ooss-u*r*l, kum.

| Corn pads, Cotton-wool. | Hühneraugenpflaster, Watte. |

hü'-ner-owg-en-pflust'-er, vutt'-e*r*.

| Eau de Cologne. | Kölnisch Wasser. |

ku*r*l'-nish vuss'-er.

| Eyeblack, Eye lotion. | Augenstift, Augenwasser |

owg'-en-shtift, owg'-en-vuss'-er.

| Face cream, Flannel. | Hautcrème, Flanell. |

howt'-craim, flun-ell'.

| Gargle, Hair oil. | Mundwasser, Haaröl. |

moont'-vuss-er, hahr'-u*r*l.

| Lint, Lipstick. | Verbandstoff, Lippenstift. |

fair-bunt'-shtoff, lip'-en-shtift.

Mirror, Nail-brush. | Spiegel, Nagelbürste.
shpee'-gel, nahg'-el-bürst-er.

Nail-file, Nail-varnish. | Nagelfeile, Nagellack.
nahg'-el-fī'-ler, nahg'-el-luck.

Nail-varnish remover. | Nagellackentferner.
nahg'-el-luck-ent-fern'-er.

Oilsilk, Ointment. | Ölhaut, Salbe.
url'-howt, zulb'-er.

Pills, Plaster. | Pillen, Pflaster.
pill'-en, Pflust'-er.

Powder (medicinal, face). | Pulver, Puder.
pool'-fer, poo'-der.

Pumice-stone. | Bimsstein.
bimss'-shtine.

Quinine. | Chinin.
chee-neen'.

Razor, blade. | Rasiermesser,
Rasierklingen.
rah-zeer'-mess-er, rah-zeer'-kling'-en.

Rouge. | Rouge.
(As in English.)

Sanitary towels. | Binden.
bin'-den.

Scissors, Soap. | Schere, Seife.
share'-er, zī'-fer.

Shaving brush, soap. | Rasierpinsel, Rasierseife.
rah-zeer'-pin-zel, rah-zeer'-zī'-fer.

Sleeping tablets. | Schlaftabletten.
shlahf'-ta-blett'-en.

Sponge, Spray. | Schwamm, Zerstäuber.
shvumm, tsair-shtoy'-ber.

Stomach-powder. | Magenpulver.
mahg'-en-pool-fer.

Sunburn-ointment, oil. | Sonnenbrandsalbe, öl.
zonn'-en-brunt-zulb'-er, url.

Sun protection cream.	Sonnenschutzcrème.
zonn'-en-shoots-kraim.	
Syringe, Towel.	Spritze, Handtuch.
shprits'-er, hunt'-tooCH.	
Talcum powder.	Talkum.
tal'-koom.	
Tooth brush, paste.	Zahnbürste, Zahnpasta.
tsahn'-bürst'-er, tsahn'-pust'-ah.	

THE HAIRDRESSER

Hairdressers in Germany, as elsewhere, are apt to decide for you what you should have done and what you should buy. One must be firm in giving instructions and declining offers. Ladies going for a shampoo are advised to take their own towel with them, as these are still scarce in Germany.

Can you recommend me a good hairdresser ?	Können Sie mir einen guten Friseur empfehlen ?
kurn'-nen zee mere i'-nen goot'-en free-zur' emp-fay'-len.	
I should like a haircut.	Ich möchte mir die Haare schneiden lassen.
ich murcht'-er mere dee hahr'-er shni'-den luss'-en.	
Shampoo and set, please.	Waschen und Legen bitte.
vush'-en oont lay'-gen bitt'-er.	
When can I come ?	Wann soll ich kommen?
vunn zoll ich komm'-en.	
I should prefer to-morrow morning (Thursday).	Ich möchte lieber morgen früh (Donnerstag) kommen.
ich murcht'-er lee'-ber morg'-en frü (donn'-ers-tahg) komm'-en.	

I want a permanent wave.	Ich möchte Dauerwellen haben.

*ich mu*rch*t'-er dow'-er-vell-en hah'-ben.*

With waves and curls.	Mit Wellen und Locken.

mit vell'-en ō͂ont lock'-en.

Trim the fringe a little.	Schneiden Sie ein biss-chen vom Pony ab.

*shnī'-den zee ine biss'-che*n *fom po'-ny up.*

Not too short.	Nicht zu kurz.

*ni*ch*t tsoo kōorts.*

Quite short.	Ganz kurz.

gunts kōorts.

Don't cut any off the top.	Schneiden Sie nichts von oben ab.

*shni'-den zee ni*ch*ts fon o'-ben up.*

Just trim it round the sides and back.	Schneiden Sie nur an den Seiten und hinten.

shnī'-den zee noor un dane zi'-ten ōͅont hin'-ten.

I part my hair on the other side, in the middle, more to the side.	Ich habe den Scheitel auf der andern Seite, in der Mitte, mehr seitwärts.

*i*ch *hah'-ber dane shī'-tel owf dair un'-dern zī'-ter, in dair mitt'-er, mair zīte'-vairts.*

Don't put any oil on.	Tun Sie kein Öl darauf.

*toon zee kine u*r*l dar-owf'.*

I like my nails pointed.	Ich möchte die Nägel spitz haben.

*i*ch *mu*rch*t'-er dee nay'-gel shpits hah'-ben.*

Please polish them.	Bitte polieren Sie sie.

bitt'-er pol-eer'-en zee zee.

Can I have a face massage ?	Kann ich eine Gesicht-massage haben ?

*kun i*ch *ī'-ne*r *gez-i*ch*t'-muss-ah'-je*r *hah'-ben.*

Curlers.	Lockenwickel.
	lock'-en-vick-el.

Hair-pins, grips.	Haarnadeln, Haarklemmen.
	hahr'-nahd-eln, hahr'-klemm-en.

Hairnet, Hair-oil.	Haarnetz, Haaröl.
	hahr'-nets, hahr'-url.

Dryer.	Föhn.
	furn.

It is too hot.	Es ist zu warm.
	ez ist tsoo var-m.

PHOTOGRAPHY

I want some films for my camera. | Ich möchte Filme für meine Kamera.
ich murcht'-er film'-er für mï'-ner kum'-er-ah.

Have you colour films ? | Haben Sie Farbfilme ?
hah'-ben zee farb'-film-er.

Do you develop films ? | Entwickeln Sie Filme ?
ent-vick'-eln zee film'-er.

One print of each. | Ein Abzug von jedem.
ine up'-tsoog fon yay'-dem.

On shiny, matt paper. | Auf Glanzpapier, mattem Papier.
owf glunts'-pup-eer', mutt'-em pup-eer'

When will they be ready ? | Wann werden sie fertig sein ?
vunn vair'-den zee fair'-tich zine.

I want them as soon as possible. | Ich möchte sie möglichst bald haben.
ich murcht'-er zee murg'-lichst bult hah'-ben.

Please enlarge these two. | Bitte vergrössern Sie diese beiden.
bitt'-er fair-grurss'-en zee dee'-zer bï'-den.

BOOKSHOP AND STATIONER

Where is the nearest, best, bookshop?	Wo ist die nächste (beste) Buchhandlung?

vo ist dee next'-er (best'-er) booCH'-hunt-loong.

Have you any English books?	Haben Sie englische Bücher?

hah'-ben zee eng'-lish-er bü*ch*'-er.

What is the latest English novel you have?	Was ist der neueste englische Roman, den Sie haben?

vuss ist dair noy'-est-er eng'-lish-er ro-mahn', dane zee hah'-ben.

Have you any of ——'s books in English?	Haben Sie ——s Bücher auf englisch?

hah'-ben zee ——s bü*ch*'-er owf eng'-lish.

In English, in German.	Auf englisch, auf deutsch.

owf eng'-lish, owf doytsh.

I want a German-English, English-German dictionary.	Ich möchte ein deutsch-englisches (englisch-deutsches) Wörterbuch.

ich mur*ch*t'-er ine doytsh-eng'-lish-ez (eng'-lish-doytsh-ez) vurt'-er-booCH.

Please give me something in very simple German.	Bitte geben Sie mir etwas in sehr einfachem Deutsch.

bitt'-er gay'-ben zee mere et'-vuss in zair ine'-faCH'-em doytsh.

Is there a paper cover, leather, cloth bound edition?	Gibt es eine geheftete (Leder, gebundene) Ausgabe?

geebt ez ī'-ner ge-hef'-tet-er (lay'-der, geb-oon-den-er) owce'-gahb'-er.

I want some writing-paper, please.	Ich möchte etwas Brief-papier, bitte.

ich murcht'-e*r* et'-vuss brief'-pup-eer bitt'-e*r*.

And envelopes.	Und Umschläge.

ŏont ŏŏm'-shlay-ge*r*.

Have you a map of Germany, of the city, of the district ?	Haben Sie eine Karte von Deutschland, (von der Stadt, von der Umgebung) ?

hah'-ben zee ī'-ne*r* kart'-e*r* fon doytsh'-lunt (fon dare shtutt, fon dair ŏŏm'-gay-bŏŏng).

Do you stock playing-cards ?	Haben Sie Spielkarten ?

hah'-ben zee shpeel'-kart-en.

Fountain-pen, Pencil.	Füller, Bleistift.

füll'-e*r*, blī'-shtift.

Pen, Nib.	Federhalter, Schreibfeder.

fay'der-hult-e*r*, shribe'-fay-der.

Propelling-pencil, Refill.	Füllbleistift, Ersatzblei.

füll'-blī-shtift, er-zuts'-blī.

Rubber, Ruler.	Radiergummi, Lineal.

rahd-eer'-goom-ee, leen-ay-ahl'.

Bottle of ink.	Eine Flasche Tinte.

ī'-ne*r* flush'-e*r* tint'-e*r*.

Paper-clips, Paste.	Heftklammer, Klebstoff.

heft'-klumm-er, klaib'-shtoff.

Brush, Scissors.	Pinsel, Schere.

pin'-zel, shay'-re*r*.

Sealing-wax.	Siegellack.

zee'-gel-luck.

THE BANK

Which is the way to the —— Bank ?	Wie komme ich zur —— Bank ?

vee komm'-er ich tsoor —— bunk.

Do you cash travellers' cheques ?	Nehmen Sie Reiseschecks ?

nay'-men zee rī'-zer-shecks.

What is the rate of exchange ?	Wie ist der Kurs ?

vee ist dair koors.

I have a letter of credit.	Ich habe einen Kredit-brief.

ich hah'-beï'-nen kray-deet'-brief.

I want to draw——	Ich möchte —— abheben.

ich murch'-ter' —— up'-hay-ben.

Can I see the manager ?	Kann ich den Vorsteher sprechen ?

kun ich dane fore'-shtay-er shprech'-en.

When shall I come back ?	Wann soll ich wieder-kommen ?

vun zol ich vee'-der-komm-en.

What time do you close ?	Wann schliessen Sie ?

vun shleess'-en zee.

I cannot wait so long.	Ich kann nicht so lange warten.

ich kun nicht zo lung'-er var'-ten.

GENERAL SHOPPING VOCABULARY

The definite article is only mentioned below to indicate the gender of the word ; where the object is always bought more than one at a time, the plural form only is given. One would say, on entering a shop, "Ich möchte (ich murch'-ter) einen Hut, ein Kleid, eine Tasche, ein Paar Schuhe, etwas (et'-vuss) Puder ("some powder"). Einen ("a") corresponds to the definite article der, ein to das, and eine to die.

Alarm clock.	Der Wecker.
	dair veck'-er.
Alpenstock.	Der Alpenstock.
	dair ulp'-en-shtock.
Attache case.	Das Stadtköfferchen.
	duss shtutt'-kurf-er-chen.
Bathing cap, Bathing suit.	Die Bademütze, Der Badeanzug.
	dee bahd'-er-müts-er, dair bahd'-er-un-tsoog.
Belt.	Der Gürtel.
	dair gürt'-el.
Blouse.	Die Bluse.
	dee bloo'-zer.
Bow-tie.	Die Schleife.
	dee shli'-fer.
Camera.	Die Kamera.
	dee kum'-er-ah.
Clothes brush.	Die Kleiderbürste.
	dee kli'-der-bürst-er.
Coat, Overcoat.	Der Rock, Mantel.
	dair rock, mun'-tel.
Collar, Lace collar.	Der Kragen, Spitzen-kragen.
	dair krahg'-en, shpits'-en-krahg-en.
Cotton.	Die Baumwolle.
	dee bowm'-voll-er.

Cotton thread.	Das Garn.
	duss garn.
Cuff links.	Manschetten-Knöpfe.
	mun-shett'-en-knurpf-er.
Dress, Woollen dress.	Das Kleid, Wollkleid.
	duss klite, voll'-klite.
Dress shirt.	Das Frackhemd.
	duss fruck'-hemt.
Evening-dress tie, waistcoat.	Die Abendkrawatte, Frackweste.
	dee ah'-bent-kra-vutt'-er, fruck'-vest-er.
Evening-gown, slippers.	Das Abendkleid, Tanzschuhe.
	duss ah'-bent-klite, tunts'-shoo-er.
Evening paper.	Die Abendzeitung.
	dee ah'-bent-tsī-tōong.
Eye-glasses, spectacles.	Die Brille.
	dee brill'-er.
Fur gloves.	Pelzhandschuhe.
	pelts'-hunt-shoo-er.
Garters.	Strumpfbänder.
	shtrōōmpf'-bend-er.
Gloves, white gloves.	Handschuhe, weisse Handschuhe.
	hunt'-shoo-er, vīss'-er hunt'-shoo-er.
Gramphone record.	Die Schallplatte.
	dee shul'-plutt-er.
Hair brush.	Die Haarbürste.
	dee hahr'-bürst-er.
Handkerchiefs	Taschentücher.
	tush'-en-tüch-er.
Hat, Headsquare.	Der Hut, Das Kopftuch.
	dair hoot, duss kopf'-tooCH.
Lipstick.	Der Lippenstift.
	dair lipp'-en-shtift.

Mirror.	Der Spiegel.
	dair shpee'-gel.
Music.	Noten.
	no'-ten.
Newspaper.	Die Zeitung.
	dee tsī'-tŏong.
Nightdress, Nightshirt.	Das Nachthemd.
	duss naCHt'-hemt.
Pants, Petticoat.	Die Unterhose, Der Unterrock.
	dee ŏŏn'-ter-ho-zer, dair ŏŏn'-ter-rock.
Pins, Powder.	Stecknadeln, Puder.
	shteck'-nahd-eln, poo'-der.
Pullover, Pyjamas.	Der Pullover, Der Schlafanzug.
	dair (as in English), dair shlahf'-un-tsoog.
Raincoat.	Der Regenmantel.
	dair ray'-gen-munt-el.
Rouge.	Das Rouge.
	duss (as in English).
Safety-pins.	Sicherheitsnadeln.
	zeech'-er-hītes-nahd-eln.
Scarf.	Der Schal.
	dair shahl.
Shirt(s).	Das Hemd, Hemden.
	duss hemt, hem'-den.
Shoes, Shoe-laces.	Schuhe, Schnürbänder.
	shoo'-er, shnür'-bend-er.
Shoe-horn, polish.	Der Schuhlöffel, Die Schuhwichse.
	dair shoo'-lurf-el, dee shoo'-vicks-er.
Silk, Skirt.	Seide, Der Rock.
	zī'-der, dair rock.
Socks, Stockings.	Socken, Strümpfe.
	zock'-en, shtrümpf'-er.

Souvenir-gifts.	Reiseandenken.
	rī'-zer-un-denk-en.
Stamps.	Briefmarken.
	brief'-mark-en.
Studs.	Hemd-Knöpfe.
	hemt'-knurp-fer.
Suit-case.	Der Handkoffer.
	dair hunt'-koff-er.
Sun-dress, Sun-glasses.	Das Sonnenkleid, Die Sonnenbrille.
	duss zonn'-en-klite, dee zonn'-en-brill-er.
Suspenders.	Der Sockenhalter (Strumpfhalter).
	dair zock'-en-hult-er (stroompf'-hult-er).
Tennis flannels, shoes.	Die Tennishose, Tennis-schuhe.
	dee tennis-ho'-zer, tennis-shoo'-er.
Tie, Trousers.	Der Schlips, Die Hose.
	dair shlipps, dee ho'-zer.
Towel.	Das Handtuch.
	duss hunt'-tooCH.
Travelling-rug.	Die Reisedecke.
	dee rī'-zer-deck-er.
Vest.	Das Unterhemd.
	duss oon'-ter-hemt.
Umbrella, Walking stick.	Der Regenschirm, Spazierstock.
	dair ray'-gen-sheerm, shputs-eer'-shtock.
Wool, Knitting-needles.	Die Wolle, Stricknadeln.
	dee voll'-er, shtrick'-nahd-eln.
Wrist-watch.	Die Armbanduhr.
	dee arm'-bunt-oor.
Zipp-fastener.	Der Reissverschluss.
	dair rice'-fair-shlooss.

This is not my size.	Das ist nicht meine Grösse.

duss ist nicht mī'-ner grurss'-er.

It is too big, small, wide, narrow, tight.	Es ist zu gross, klein, weit, schmal, eng.

ez ist tsoo grōss, kline, vite, shmahl, eng.

With short, long sleeves.	Mit kurzen (langen) Ärmeln.

mit kŏŏrts'-en (lung'-en) erm'-eln.

That is not what I want.	Das ist nicht was ich will.

duss ist nicht vuss ich vill.

I do not like the colour.	Die Farbe gefällt mir nicht.

dee far'-ber gef-ellt' mere nicht.

I prefer a darker, lighter colour.	Ich möchte eine dunklere (hellere) Farbe haben.

ich murch'-ter i'-ner dŏŏnk'-ler-er (hell'-er-er) far'-ber hah'-ben.

That will fade.	Es wird verblassen.

ez virt fair-bluss'-en.

Does this material shrink ?	Geht dieser Stoff ein ?

gate dee'-zer shtoff ine.

Is it waterproof ?	Ist er wasserdicht ?

ist air vuss'-er-dicht.

Will these gloves wash ?	Kann man diese Handschuhe waschen ?

kun mun dee'-zer hunt'-shoo-er vush'-en.

May I try this on ?	Darf ich das anprobieren ?

darf ich duss un'-pro-beer-en.

It does not fit me.	Es passt mir nicht.

ez pust mere nicht.

| That is too fancy; I want something quite simple. | Das ist zu bunt; ich will etwas ganz Einfaches. |

duss ist tsoo bŏŏnt ; ich vill et'-vuss gunts ine'-faCH-es.

| That is too dear. | Das ist zu teuer. |

duss ist tsoo toy'-er.

| Is that the cheapest you have? | Ist das das Billigste, das Sie haben? |

ist duss duss bill'-ich-ster, duss zee hah'-ben.

| I want a better quality. | Ich möchte eine bessere Qualität. |

ich murch'-ter i'-ner bess'-er-er k-vul-ee-tait.

| I do not mind paying a little more. | Ich würde etwas mehr zahlen. |

ich vürd'-er et'-vuss mair tsahl'-en.

| May I see this by daylight? | Darf ich das bei Tageslicht sehen? |

darf ich duss by tahg'-ez-licht zay'-en.

| Let me look in the mirror. | Lassen Sie mich in den Spiegel sehen. |

luss'-en zee mich in dane shpee'-gel zay'-en.

| Have you nothing better? | Haben Sie nichts Besseres? |

hah'-ben zee nichts bess'-er-ez.

| What do you charge for making one? | Was kostet es, wenn Sie es anfertigen? |

vuss kost'-et ez, venn zee ez un'-fair-tig-en.

| When could I have it? | Wann könnte ich es haben? |

vunn kurn'-ter ich ez hah'-ben.

| Can you take it in at the waist? | Können Sie es an der Taille enger machen? |

kurn'-en zee ez un dair ti'-yer eng'-er maCH'-en.

| I will take it with me. | Ich nehme es mit. |

ich nay'-mer ez mit.

| Please send it. | Bitte schicken Sie es. |

bitt'-er shick'-en zee ez.

| How much is it alto-gether ? | Was macht es zusamm-en ? |

vuss maCHt ez tsoo-zum'-en.

| I will pay on delivery. | Ich werde bei Abliefer-ung zahlen. |

ich vair'-der by up'-leef-er-ŏong tsahl'-en.

| I have not enough money with me. | Ich habe nicht genug Geld bei mir. |

ich hah'-ber nicht gen-ooCH gelt by mere.

REPAIRS

| I must take these shoes to the shoemaker. | Ich muss diese Schuhe zum Schuster bringen. |

ich mŏoss dee'-zer shoo'-er tsŏom shŏost'-er bring'-en.

| I need new soles, and heels. | Ich brauche neue Sohlen (und Absätze). |

ich browCH'-er noy'-er zō'-len ŏont up'-zets-er.

| When will they be ready ? | Wann werden sie fertig sein ? |

vunn vair'-den zee fair'-tich zine.

| I have broken my glasses. | Meine Brille ist kaputt. |

mī'-ner brill'-er ist ka-pŏot'.

| I need a new lens, frame, bridge. | Ich brauche ein neues Glas, eine Fassung, einen Steg. |

ich browCH'-er ine noy'-ez gluss, ī'-ner fuss'-ŏong, ī'-nen shtaig.

| That is too tight, slack. | Das ist zu fest, lose. |

duss ist tsoo fest, lo'-zer.

| That is not straight. | Das ist nicht gerade. |

duss ist nicht ger-ahd'-er.

I want some dark glasses made with the same lenses.	Ich möchte dunkle Gläser in derselben Schärfe haben.

ich murcht'-er dŏŏnk'-ler glay'-zer in dair-zelb'-en sherf'-er hah'-ben.

My watch has stopped, is broken.	Meine Uhr ist stehengeblieben, ist kaputt.

mi'-ner oor ist shtay'-en-geb-lee'-ben, ist ka-pŏŏt'.

My watch needs cleaning.	Meine Uhr muss gereinigt werden.

mi'-ner oor mŏŏss ger-i'-nicht vair'-den.

It gains, loses.	Sie geht vor, geht nach.

zee gate fore, gate naCH.

Please regulate it.	Bitte regulieren Sie sie.

bitt'-er reg-oo-leer'-en zee zee.

The hand has come off.	Der Zeiger ist abgebrochen.

dair tsi'-ger ist up'-geb-roCH-en.

I have lost the hand.	Ich habe den Zeiger verloren.

ich hah'-ber dane tsi'-ger fair-lō'-ren.

The spring is broken.	Die Feder ist kaputt

dee fay'-der ist ka-pŏŏt'.

I overwound it.	Ich habe sie überdreht.

ich hah'-ber zee ü-ber-drait'.

Give me a new strap, please.	Geben Sie mir ein neues Band bitte.

gay'-ben zee mere ine noy'-ez bunt bitt'-er.

Can you repair my camera for me?	Können Sie mir die Kamera reparieren?

kurn'-en zee mere dee kum'-er-ah rep-ar-eer'-en.

The shutter does not work.	Der Verschluss funktioniert nicht.

dair fair-shlŏŏss' fŏŏnk-tsee-on-eert' nicht.

G.

D

The film does not wind properly.	Der Film dreht sich nicht richtig.

dair film drait si*ch* ni*ch*t ri*ch*'-ti*ch*.

I dropped it.	Ich habe sie fallen lassen.

i*ch* hah'-ber zee fal'-en luss'-en.

The lock on my case is broken.	Das Schloss an meinem Koffer ist kaputt.

duss shloss un mī'-nem koff'-er ist ka-pōōt'.

Can you mend it ?	Können Sie es repar-ieren ?

ku*r*n'-en zee ez rep-ar-eer'-en.

I want a new strap.	Ich brauche einen neuen Riemen.

i*ch* browCH'-er ī'-nen noy'-en ree'-men.

How long will it take ?	Wie lange wird es dauern ?

vee lung'-er virt ez dow'-ern.

Can you have it ready for this evening ?	Können Sie es bis heute abend machen ?

ku*r*n'-en zee ez biss hoy'-ter ah'-bent maCH'-en.

When shall I collect it ?	Wann soll ich es abholen ?

vunn zoll i*ch* ez up'-hole-en.

THE POLICE

Travellers are usually required to register with the police, and care should be taken to comply with current regulations in this matter. If you are staying for only a day or two it may not be necessary, but in any case the hotel management or landlord will know what is required. Be sure to take your passport with you when you go to register.

Where is the police station?	Wo ist das Polizeiamt?
vo ist duss pol-its-ī'-umt.	
I am British.	Ich bin Engländer.
ich bin eng'-lend-er.	
I wish to register as a foreign visitor.	Ich möchte mich als Ausländer anmelden.
ich murcht'-er mich ulce owce'-lend-er un'-meld-en.	
I am staying with —— (at the —— Hotel).	Ich wohne bei —— (im Hotel ——).
ich vō'-ner by —— (im ho-tell' ——).	
I intend to stay two months.	Ich beabsichtige, zwei Monate zu bleiben.
ich ber-up'-zich-tig-er, tsvī mō'-naht-er tsoo blī'-ben.	
Have I to inform you when I am leaving?	Muss ich mich abmelden, wenn ich abreise?
mōoss ich mich up'-meld-en, venn ich up'-rī'-zer.	
I have lost ——.	Ich habe —— verloren.
ich hah'-ber —— fair-lō'-ren.	
Is it any use advertising?	Hat es Zweck, zu inserieren?
hut ez tsveck, tsoo in-sair-eer'-en.	
Will you telephone me if it is found?	Würden Sie mich bitte anrufen, wenn es gefunden wird?
vürd'-en zee mich bitt'-er un'-roof-en, venn ez gef-ōönd'-en virt.	
Here is the reward.	Hier ist die Belohnung.
here ist dee bel-o'-nōong.	

ACCIDENT AND ILLNESS

See also " The Chemist," pages 80-84.

Send for a policeman, doctor, ambulance.	Rufen Sie einen Schutzmann, Arzt, Krankenwagen.

roof'-en zee i'-nen shoots'-mun, artst, krunk'-en-vahg'-en.

Are you all right ?	Sind Sie unverletzt ?

zint zee ŏŏn'-fair-letst.

It was (not) my fault.	Es war (nicht) meine Schuld.

ez var (nicht) mī'-ner shŏŏlt.

I did not look.	Ich habe nicht hingesehen.

ich hah'-ber nicht hin'-gez-ay-en.

He did not see me.	Er hat mich nicht gesehen.

air hut mich nicht gez-ay'-en.

Can anyone speak English ?	Spricht jemand englisch ?

shpricht yay'-munt eng'-lish.

I do not understand.	Ich verstehe nicht.

ich fair-shtay'-er nicht.

I feel better now.	Es geht mir besser.

ez gate mere bess'-er.

Can you get me some brandy ?	Können Sie mir etwas Cognac besorgen ?

kurn'-en zee mere et'-vuss con'-yac be-zorg'-en.

It's all right ; I am only shaken, bruised.	Es macht nichts ; ich habe mich nur erschrocken, gestossen.

ez maCHt nichts ; ich hah'-ber mich nŏŏr air-shrock'-en, gesh-tō'-sen.

I just want to sit down for a while.	Ich will mich nur etwas hinsetzen.

ich vill mi*ch* noor et'-vuss hin'-zets-en.

Where is the nearest doctor, chemist?	Wo ist der nächste Arzt, die nächste Apotheke?

vo ist dair next'-er artst, dee next'-er up-ō-tay'-ker.

I want to have this part dressed.	Ich möchte diese Stelle verbunden haben.

ich mur*ch*t'-er dee'-zer shtell'-er fair-bōōnd'-en hah'-ben.

Please take this; I am deeply grateful to you.	Bitte nehmen Sie das; ich bin Ihnen sehr dankbar.

bitt'-er nay'-men zee duss; *ich* bin ee'-nen zair dunk'-bar.

My leg is very painful.	Das Bein tut sehr weh.

duss bine toot zair vay.

It hurts me here.	Es tut mir hier weh.

ez toot mere here vay.

I can't move.	Ich kann mich nicht bewegen.

ich kun mi*ch* ni*ch*t bev-ay'-gen.

I have a pain in the small of my back.	Ich habe Schmerzen im Kreuz.

ich hah'-ber shmairts'-en im kroyts.

I have broken my ankle.	Ich habe den Knöchel gebrochen.

ich hah'-ber dane k-nur*ch*'-el geb-roCH'-en.

I have cut my wrist.	Ich habe mir das Handgelenk zerschnitten.

ich hah'-ber mere duss hunt'-gel enk tsair-shnitt'-en.

I have burnt my hand.	Ich habe mir die Hand verbrannt.

ich hah'-ber mere dee hunt fair-brunt.

I've a nasty cut on the head.	Ich habe einen schlimmen Schnitt auf dem Kopf.

ich hah'-ber ī'-nen shlimm'-en shnitt owf dame kopf.

Put some iodine on this cut ; there may be some glass in it.	Geben Sie Jod auf die Wunde ; vielleicht ist Glas hineingekommen

gay'-ben zee yote owf dee voond'-er ; feel-licht' ist gluss hin-ine'-gek-omm-en.

I feel faint.	Ich fühle mich schwach.

ich fü'-ler mich shvaCH.

Have you any smelling-salts ?	Haben Sie Riechsalz ?

hah'-ben zee reech'-zults.

I have a bad cold.	Ich bin sehr erkältet.

ich bin zair air-kelt'-et.

I have a sore throat, headache, influenza.	Ich habe Halsschmerzen, Kopfschmerzen, Influenza.

ich hah'-ber hulce'-shmairts-en, kopf'-shmairts-en, influenza.

Can I get up, or must I stay in bed ?	Kann ich aufstehen, oder muss ich im Bett bleiben ?

knn ich owf'-shtay-en, ŏ'-der mŏŏss ich im bett blī'-ben.

How long must I stay in bed ?	Wie lange muss ich im Bett bleiben ?

vee lung'-er mŏŏss ich im bett blī'-ben.

Can you get me a nurse ?	Können Sie mir eine Pflegerin verschaffen.

kurn'-en zee mere i'-ner pflay'-ger-in fair-shuff'-en.

Shall I be fit to travel on Wednesday ?	Werde ich Mittwoch reisen können ?

vair'-der ich mitt'-voCH rī'-zen kurn'-en.

When will you come again ?	Wann kommen Sie wieder ?

vun komm'-en zee vee'-der.

I think I'm all right now.	Ich glaube ich bin jetzt wieder gesund.

ich glow'-ber ich bin yetst vee'-der gez-ŏŏnt'.

AT THE DENTIST'S

Can you recommend me a good dentist ?	Können Sie mir einen guten Zahnarzt empfehlen ?

kurn'-en zee mere i'-nen goot'-en tsahn'-artst emp-fay'-len.

What is his address ?	Wo wohnt er ?

vo vönt air.

I have terrible toothache.	Ich habe schreckliche Zahnschmerzen.

ich hah'-ber shreck'-lich-er tsahn'-shmairts-en.

I have had it for three days now.	Ich habe sie schon seit drei Tagen.

ich hah'ber zee shone zite dry tahg'-en.

I don't know what is the matter.	Ich weiss nicht was los ist.

ich vice nicht vuss loce ist.

I have lost a stopping.	Ich habe eine Plombe verloren.

ich hah'-ber i'-ner plom'-ber fair-lö'-ren.

The nerve hurts.	Der Nerv tut weh.

dair nairf toot vay.

The gums are so sore.	Das Zahnfleisch tut so weh.

duss tsahn'-flīsh toot zo vay.

I want to have this tooth out.	Ich will diesen Zahn gezogen haben.

ich vill dee'-zen tsahn ger-tsö'-gen hah'-ben.

Must it come out ?	Ist es notwendig, ihn zu ziehen ?

ist ez note'-vend-ich, een tsoo tsee'-en.

I want this tooth filled.	Ich möchte diesen Zahn plombiert haben.

ich murcht'-er dee'-zen tsahn plom-beert' hah'-ben.

I should like it temporarily stopped.	Ich möchte ihn vorübergehend gefüllt haben.

ich murcht'-er een for-ü-ber-gay-ent gef-üllt' hah'-ben.

Filling.	Plombe, Füllung.

plom'-ber, füll'-ŏong.

Gold crown, Plate.	Goldkrone, Platte.

golt'-krō-ner, plutt'-er.

Please be gentle.	Bitte seien Sie vorsichtig.

bitt'-er zī'-en zee fore'-zich-tich.

It is very painful.	Es tut sehr weh.

ez toot zair vay.

That hurts.	Das tut weh.

duss toot vay.

Am I to come again ?	Muss ich wiederkommen ?

mŏoss ich vee'-der-komm-en.

I am leaving here on the——	Ich reise am —— ab.

ich rī'-zer um — up.

That is much better.	Das ist viel besser.

duss ist feel bess'-er.

I hope that will be all right now.	Ich hoffe, es wird jetzt gut sein.

ich hoff'-er, ez virt yetst goot zine.

How much is that ?	Was kostet das ?

vuss kost'-et duss.

AT TABLE

See note on Rationing in Introduction, page 11.

Where is the restaurant ?	Wo ist das Restaurant ?

vo ist duss rest'-or-ong.

Will you order a table for four ?	Würden Sie einen Tisch für vier Personen bestellen ?

vürd'-en zee ī'-nen tish für feer pair-zō'-nen ber-shtell'-en.

Where can I have a wash ?	Wo kann ich mich waschen ?

vo kun ich mich vush'-en.

Can we have breakfast in the bedroom, or only downstairs ?	Können wir Frühstück im Zimmer haben, oder nur unten ?

kurn'-en vere frü'-shtük im tsimm'-er hah'-ben, ō'-der noor ōōn'-ten.

Tea for one and coffee for three.	Einmal Tee und dreimal Kaffee.

ine'-mahl tay ōōnt dry'-mahl kuff'-ay.

Bring us three rolls each and some butter.	Bringen Sie uns je drei Brötchen und Butter.

bring'-en zee ōōns yay dry brurt'-chen ōōnt bōōt'-er.

I should like some marmalade.	Ich hätte gern etwas Orangenmarmelade.

ich hett'-er gairn et'-vuss or-un'-jen-mar-mel-ahd'-er.

Have you any honey or jam ?	Haben Sie Honig oder Marmelade ?

hah'-ben zee ho'-nich o'der mar-mel-ahd'-er.

Bring some more toast.	Bringen Sie noch etwas Toast.

bring'-en zee noCH et'-vuss toast (as in English).

Is there a table d'hôte ?	Gibt es table d'hôte ?

geebt ez table d'hôte (as in French).

We will order à la carte.	Wir bestellen à la carte.

vere be*r*-shtell'-en à la carte (as in French).

Please serve us quickly, we have to catch a train, we are going to the theatre.	Bitte bedienen Sie uns schnell, wir müssen zur Bahn (wir wollen ins Theater).

bitt'-e*r* bed-een'-en zee ŏŏns shnell, vere müss'-en tsoor bahn (vere voll'-en inz tay-aht'-e*r*).

Bring me the menu, the wine-list.	Bringen Sie mir die Speisekarte, die Weinkarte.

bring'-en zee mere dee shpī'-ze*r*-kart-e*r* (dee vine'-kart-e*r*).

Can you recommend a good local wine ?	Können Sie einen guten Wein aus der Umgegend empfehlen ?

kurn'-en zee ī'-nen goot'-en vine owce dair ŏŏm'-gayg-ent emp-fay'-len.

What is that called in German ?	Wie heisst das auf deutsch ?

vee hīsst duss owf doytsh.

Between what times is dinner served ?	Um welche Zeit wird das Abendessen serviert ?

oom vel*ch*'-e*r* tsite virt duss ah'-bent-ess-en sair-veert'.

Can I have a table at the window ?	Kann ich einen Tisch am Fenster haben ?

kun i*ch* ī'-nen tish um fen'-ster hah'-ben.

Can one have tea in the lounge ?	Kann man Tee in der Halle haben ?

kun mun tay in dair hull'-e*r* hah'-ben.

I will take my coffee in the lounge.	Ich will Kaffee in der Halle haben.

i*ch* vill kuff'-ay in dair hull'-e*r* hah'-ben.

Waiter !	Herr Ober !

hair ō'-ber.

| Ask the head waiter to come over here. | Rufen Sie den Ober-kellner. |

roof'-en zee dane ō'-ber-kell-ner.

| The plates are cold. | Die Teller sind kalt. |

dee tell'-er zint kult.

| This is not properly cooked. | Das ist nicht richtig gekocht. |

duss ist nicht rich'-tich ger-koCHt'.

| I like it underdone, well done. | Ich möchte es halbgeb-raten, gut gebraten. |

ich murch'-ter ez hulp'-geb-raht'-en, goot geb-raht'-en.

| Bring me another help-ing. | Geben Sie mir noch eine Portion. |

gay'-ben zee mere noCH i'-ner por-tsee-ōn'.

| No, thank you, I have had enough. | Danke, ich habe genug gehabt. |

dunk'-er, ich hah'-ber ger-nōōCH ger-hubt'.

| Yes, please. | Ja, bitte. |

yah, bitt'-er

"Danke" means "No, thank you"; if you wish to say "Yes, thank you," it is "Bitte" or "Ja, bitte."

| Bring me another spoon, knife, fork. | Bringen Sie mir noch einen Löffel, ein Mess-er, eine Gabel. |

bring'-en zee mere noCH i'-nen lurf'-el, ine mess'-er, i'-ner gahb'-el

| A glass of iced water, please. | Ein Glas Eiswasser bitte. |

ine gluss ice'-vuss-er bitt'-er.

| I prefer the leg, wing, breast. | Ich möchte Bein, Flügel, Brust haben. |

ich murch'-ter bine, flü'-gel, brōōst hah'-ben.

Bill, please.	Zahlen bitte.

tsah'-len bitt'-er.

Is that with service included ?	Ist die Bedienung einbegriffen ?

ist dee bed-een'-ŏong ine'-beg-riff-en.

This is not correct.	Das stimmt nicht.

duss shtimmt nicht.

MENU AND UTENSILS

The definite article is given with each word to indicate the gender. In the case of words given in the plural, the definite article (" die " for all genders) is omitted.

Apple, apples.	Der Apfel, Äpfel.

dair up'fel, ep'-fel.

Apricots, Asparagus.	Aprikosen, der Spargel.

Ap-ri-kose'-en, dair shpar'-gel.

Bacon (fried bacon).	der Speck (gebratener Speck).

dair shpeck, (ge-braht'-en-er shpeck).

Bacon and eggs.	Spiegeleier mit Speck.

shpee'-gel-i-er mit shpeck.

Black pudding.	Die Blutwurst.

dee bloot'-vŏorst.

Beans (French).	Bohnen (grüne).

bo'-nen (grü'-ner).

Beans (broad).	Bohnen (weisse).

bo'-nen (vice'-er).

Beef (boiled).	Das Rindfleisch (gekochtes).

duss rint'-flish (ge-koCH'-tez).

Beef (roast).	Der Rinderbraten.

dair rinn'-der-braht-en.

Beer, Lager.	Das Bier, Das Lagerbier.

duss beer, duss lah'-ger-beer.

Biscuit, Brandy. | Das Keks, Der Cognac.
duss cakes, dair con'-yac.

Bread (white, brown). | Das Brot (weiss, schwarz).
duss broat (vice, shvar'-ts).

Burgundy, Butter. | Der Burgunder, Die Butter.
dair boor-goon'-der, dee boot'-er.

Cabbage. | Der Weisskohl.
dair vice'-coal.

Cake. | Der Kuchen.
dair kooCH'-en.

Fancy cake (in Switzer- | Die Patisserie.
land).
dee pa-teess'-er-ee'.

Calf's head, liver. | Der Kalbskopf, Die Kalbsleber.
dair kulps'-kopf, dee kulps'-lay-ber.

Carrots. | Karotten, or Möhren.
kar-ott'-en, mur'-ren.

Cauliflower, Caviar. | Der Blumenkohl, Der Kaviar.
dair bloo'-men-coal, dair cav-ee-ahr'.

Celery, Cheese. | Die Sellerie, Der Käse.
dee zell'-er-ee, dair kay'-zer.

Chicken, Chocolate. | Das Huhn, die Schokolade.
duss hoon, dee shock-o-lahd'-er.

Chop (mutton). | Die Hammelrippe.
dee hum'-el-ripp-er.

Cider, Cod. | Der Apfelwein, Der Kabeljau.
dair up'-fel-vine, dair kah'-bel-yow.

Coffee, Cream. | Der Kaffee, Der Rahm (or, Die Sahne).
dair kuff'-ay, dair rahm (dee zahn'-er.)

Cold Meat.	Kaltes Fleisch.

kult'-ez flīsh.

Cucumber (salad).	Die Gurke, Der Gurken- salat.

dee goor'-ker, dair goor'-ken-zul-aht'.

Cup (tea, coffee).	Die Tasse (Teetasse, Kaffeetasse.

dee tuss'-er (tay'-tuss-er, kuff'-ay-tuss-er).

Custard, Cutlet.	Der Pudding, Die Kote- lette.

dair pudding (as in English), dee cot-let'.

Dessert.	Der Nachtisch.

dair naCH'-tish.

Dinner (evening).	Das Abendessen.

duss ah'-bent-ess-en.

Dinner (midday).	Das Mittagessen.

duss mit'-ahg-ess-en.

Dried egg, Dried milk.	Das Eipulver, Milch- pulver.

duss ī'-pool-fer, milch'-pool-fer.

Duck.	Die Ente.

dee ent'-er.

Egg(s) (boiled soft, hard).	Weich (hart) gekochte(s) Ei(er).

vīch (hart) ger-koCH'-te (z) ī' (-er).

Eggs, fried (Scrambled eggs).	Spiegeleier, (Rühreier).

shpee'-gel-ī-er (rür'-i-er).

Fillet of veal, Fish.	Das Kalbsfilet, Der Fisch.

duss kulps-fill-ay', dair fish.

Fork, Fruit.	Die Gabel, Das Obst.

dee gah'-bel, duss ōbst.

Fruit tart.	Die Obsttorte.

dee ōbst'-tort-er.

| Gin, Grapes. | Der Wacholder, Weintrauben. |

dair vaCH-oll'-der, vine'-trow-ben.

| Gravy, Ham. | Die Sosse, Der Schinken. |

dee zōss'-er, dair shink'-en.

| Herring, Haddock. | Der Hering, Der Schellfisch. |

dair hair'-ing, dair shell'-fish.

| Hake, Halibut. | Der Hecht, Der Heilbutt. |

dair hecht, dair hile'-boot.

| Hock. | Der (weisse) Rheinwein. |

dair (vice'-er) rine-vine.

| Ice, Ice-cream. | Das Eis. |

duss ice.

| Jam. | Eingemachtes, Die Marmelade. |

ine'-gem-aCHt'-ez, dee mar-mel-ahd'-er.

| Kidney, Knife. | Die Niere, Das Messer. |

dee neer'-er, duss mess'-er.

| Lamb, Liver. | Das Lammfleisch, Die Leber. |

duss lumm'-flīsh, dee lay'-ber.

| Lemon, Lemonade. | Die Zitrone, Die Limonade. |

dee tsee-trō'-ner, dee lee-mon-ahd'-er.

| Leek, Lettuce. | Der Lauch, Der Kopfsalat. |

dair lowCH, dair kopf'-zul-aht'.

| Liqueur, Lobster. | Der Likör, Der Hummer. |

dair leek-urr', dair hoŏm'-er.

| Lunch (cold). | Das Mittagessen (kaltes). |

duss mit'-ahg-ess-en (kult'-ez).

Marmalade. | Die Orangen-
| Marmelade.

dee o-rong'-jen-mar-mel-ahd'-er.

Melon, Milk. | Die Melone, Die Milch.

dee may-loan'-er, dee milch.

Mineral water. | Das Mineralwasser.

duss min-er-ahl'-vuss-er.

Mushrooms, Mutton. | Pilze, Das Hammel-
| fleisch.

pilts'-er, duss humm'-el-flīsh.

Mustard. | Der Senf.

dair zenf.

Napkin. | Die Serviette.

dee zer-vee-ett'-er.

Olives, Oil. | Oliven, Das Öl.

ol-eev'-en, duss url.

Omelette, Onion. | Die Omelette, Die
| Zwiebel.

dee om-let', dee tsvee'-bel.

Orange, Oysters. | Die Apfelsine, Austern.

dee up-fel-zee'-ner, owce'-tern.

Partridge, Paste. | Das Rebhuhn, Der Teig.

duss rape'-hoon, dair tīg.

Peach, Pear. | Der Pfirsich, Die Birne.

dair pfeer'-zich, dee beer'-ner.

Peas, Pea-soup. | Erbsen, Die Erbsen-
| suppe.

airb'-zen, dee airb'-zen-zoop'-er.

Pepper, Pheasant. | Der Pfeffer, Der Fasan·

dair pfeff'-er, dair fa-zahn'.

Pie, Pineapple. | Die Pastete, Die Ananas.

dee pus-tay'-ter, dee un'-un-uss.

Plate, Soup-plate. | Der Teller, Suppen-
| teller.

dair tell'-er, zoop'-en-tell-er.

| Plum, Plum-tart. | Die Pflaume, Der Pflaumenauflauf. |

dee pflow'-mer, dair pflow'-men-owf-lowf.

| Pork, Port. | Das Schweinefleisch, Der Portwein. |

duss shvine'-er-flish, dair port-vine.

| Potatoes (fried). | Kartoffeln (Bratkartoffeln). |

kar-toff'-eln (braht'-kar-toff'-eln).

| Poultry, Prunes. | Das Geflügel, Backpflaumen. |

duss ger-flü'-gel, buck'-pflow-men.

| Hors d'œuvres. | Die Vorspeise. |

dee fore'-shpī-zer.

| Rabbit, Radish. | Das Kaninchen, Das Radieschen. |

duss kun-een'-chen, duss ra-deess'-chen.

| Ragout, Raspberries. | Das Ragout, Himbeeren. |

duss ra-goo', him'-bair-en.

| Rhubarb, Rice. | Der Rhabarber, Der Reis. |

dair ra-barb'-er, dair rice.

| Roasted. | Geröstet, Gebraten. |

ger-rurst'-et, geb-raht'-en.

| Roll. | Das Brötchen, Die Semmel. |

duss brurt'-chen, dee zemm'-el.

| Salad, Salt. | Der Salat, Das Salz. |

dair zul-aht', duss Zults.

| Salmon, Sardines in oil. | Der Lachs, Ölsardinen. |

dair lucks, url'-zar-deen'-nen.

| Sandwich. | Das belegte Brot. |

duss bel-ayg'-ter broat.

Sauce, Saucer.	Die Sosse, Die Unter-tasse.

dee zoss'-e*r*, dee ŏŏnt'-er-tuss-e*r*.

Sausage, Sherry.	Die Wurst, Der Sherry.

dee voorst, dair sherry.

Soda, Sole.	Das Soda, Die Scholle.

duss zo'-dah, dee sholl'-e*r*.

Soup, gravy.	Die Suppe, Die Kraft-brühe.

dee zŏŏp'-e*r*, dee kruft'-brü-e*r*.

Soup, clear (thick).	Die Bouillon, Suppe mit Einlage.

dee boo-yong', zŏŏp'-e*r* mit ine'-lahg-e*r*.

Spinach.	Der Spinat.

dair shpee-naht'.

Spoon, table (tea).	Der Esslöffel (Teelöffel).

dair ess'-lu*r*f-el (tay'-lu*r*f-el).

Stewed fruit.	Das Kompott.

duss kom-pot'.

Strawberries (and cream).	Erdbeeren (mit Sahne).

airt'-bair-en (mit zahn'-e*r*).

Sugar, Supper.	Der Zucker, Das Abend-essen.

dair tsŏŏk'-er, duss ah'-bent-ess-en.

Sweets.	Süssigkeiten, Pralines.

züss'-ich-kite-en, prahl'-een-ay.

Table, Table-cloth.	Der Tisch, Das Tisch-tuch.

dair tish, duss tish'-tooCH.

Tea, Tea-pot.	Der Tee, Die Teekanne.

dair tay, dee tay'-kunn-e*r*.

Toast, Tongue.	Der Toast, Die Zunge.

dair toast, dee tsŏŏng'-e*r*.

Tomato.	Die Tomate.
	dee tō-maht'-er.

Toothpick, Truffles.	Der Zahnstocher, Trüffeln.
	dair tsahn'-shtoCH-er, trüff'-eln.

Turkey, Turnip.	Der Truthahn, Die Rübe.
	dair troot'-hahn, dee rü'-ber.

Veal, Vegetable.	Das Kalbfleisch, Das Gemüse.
	duss kulp'-flīsh, duss ger-mü'-zer.

Vegetable marrow.	Der Kürbis.
	dair kür'-biss.

Vinegar, Walnut.	Der Essig, Die Walnuss.
	dair ess'-ich, dee vul'-nooss.

Water, Whisky.	Das Wasser, Der Whisky.
	duss vuss'-er, dair whisky.

Wine, a bottle of wine.	Der Wein, Eine Flasche Wein.
	dair vine, ī'-ner flush'-er vine.

Red wine, White wine.	Der Rotwein, Der Weisswein.
	dair rote'-vine, dair vice'-vine.

Wine, a glass of.	Ein Glas Wein.
	ine gluss vine.

ENTERTAINMENT

(*See also Introduction.*) *Cinema tickets are usually purchased in advance. This is the only way of obtaining a good seat, or indeed any seat, in the case of a popular film. Smoking is forbidden in cinemas as well as in theatres. Cinema performances are not continuous, so it is advisable to find out when the film starts and get in at the beginning. Special late transport is often run for the benefit of cinema and theatre-goers. Make inquiries beforehand if you wish to use these services, as the routes may be different from the normal runs.*

At which theatre are they playing——? | In welchem Theater wird——gespielt?

in vel*ch*'-em tay-aht'-er virt —— gesh-peelt'.

What time does it start? | Wann fängt es an?

vunn fengt ez un.

When does it finish? | Wann ist es aus?

vunn ist ez owce.

Can I get something to eat at the theatre? | Kann ich im Theater etwas zu essen bekommen?

kun i*ch* im tay-aht'-er et'-vuss tsoo ess'-en bek-omm'-en.

Where can I have a meal after the theatre? | Wo kann ich nach dem Theater essen?

vo kun i*ch* naCH dame tay-aht'-er ess'-en.

When is the last tram, bus? | Wann fährt die letzte Strassenbahn, der letzte Omnibus?

vunn fairt dee lets'-ter shtrahss'-en-bahn, dair lets'-ter omm'-ni-booss.

Is there a special tram to —— after the theatre? | Fährt eine Theaterbahn nach——?

fairt i'-ner tay-aht'-er-bahn naCH ——

Two good stalls, please. | Zwei gute Parkettplätze bitte.

tsvī goot'-er park-ett'-plets-er bitt'-er.

| Two circle. | Zwei erster Rang. |
| | *tsvī airst'-er rung.* |

| Have you anything better, cheaper ? | Haben Sie etwas Besseres, Billigeres ? |
| | *hah'-ben zee et'-vuss bess'-er-ez, bill'-ig-er-ez.* |

| Shall I see, hear well from there ? | Werde ich von da aus gut sehen, hören ? |
| | *vair'-der ich fon dah owce goot zay'-en, hur'-ren.* |

| Those are too near the orchestra. | Diese sind zu nahe am Orchester. |
| | *dee'-zer zint tsoo nah'-er um or-kest'-er.* |

| I'll take these. | Ich nehme diese. |
| | *ich nay'mer dee'-zer.* |

| Can I get an English, German text ? | Kann ich einen englischen, einen deutschen Text bekommen ? |
| | *kun ich ī'-nen eng'-lish-en, doytsh'-en text bek-omm'-en.* |

| Give me a programme, please. | Geben Sie mir ein Programm, bitte. |
| | *gay'-ben zee mere ine pro-grumm' bitt'-er.* |

| How much is it ? | Was kostet es ? |
| | *vuss kost'-et ez ?* |

| I have no change. | Ich habe kein Kleingeld. |
| | *ich hah'-ber kine kline'-gelt.* |

| Can I hire opera-glasses? | Kann ich ein Opernglas ausleihen ? |
| | *kun ich ine o'-pern-gluss owce'-lī-en.* |

| When is the interval ? | Wann ist die Pause ? |
| | *vun ist dee pow'-zer.* |

| How long are the intervals ? | Wie lange dauern die Pausen ? |
| | *vee lung'-er dow'-ern dee pow'-zen.* |

| Are there any good films on ? | Gibt es einen guten Film ? |
| | *geebt ez ī'-nen goot'-en film.* |

| Where is the cinema? | Wo ist das Kino? |
| | |

vo ist duss keen'-o.

| I should like to see an American film. | Ich möchte gern einen amerikanischen Film sehen. |
| | |

ich murcht'-er gairn i'-nen um-air-ik-ahn'-ish-en film zay'-en.

| When does the film begin? | Wann fängt der Film an? |
| | |

vunn fengt dair film un.

| Not so near. | Nicht so nahe. |
| | |

nicht zo nah'-er.

| No smoking is allowed. | Rauchen ist nicht gestattet. |
| | |

rowCH'-en ist nicht gesh-tutt'-et.

| Which is the way out? | Wo ist der Ausgang? |
| | |

vo ist dair owce'-gung.

| Did you enjoy it? | Hat es Ihnen gefallen? |
| | |

hut ez ee'-nen gef-ul'-en.

| Let us go and have supper now. | Gehen wir jetzt essen. |
| | |

gay'-en vere yetst ess'-en.

| I should like to dance. | Ich möchte gern tanzen. |
| | |

ich murcht'-er gairn tunts'-en.

| Will you dance with me? | Würden Sie mit mir tanzen? |
| | |

vürd'-en zee mit mere tunts'-en.

| Do you tango, rumba? | Tanzen Sie Tango, (Rumba)? |
| | |

tunts'-en zee tung'-o (Room'-ba).

| I prefer a slow waltz. | Ich tanze lieber einen langsamen Walzer. |
| | |

ich tunts'-er lee'-ber i'-nen lung'-zahm-en vults'-er.

| The band plays too fast. | Die Kapelle spielt zu schnell. |
| | |

dee kup-ell'-er shpeelt tsoo shnell.

| The band is excellent. | Die Kapelle ist ausge-zeichnet. |

dee kup-ell'-er ist owce'-ger-tsïch-net.

| What is the name of that tune ? | Wie heisst dieses Lied ? |

vee hïsst dee'-zez leet.

| Will you have something to drink, eat ? | Möchten Sie etwas trinken (essen) ? |

murcht'-en zee et'-vuss trink'-en (ess'-en).

| Let us dance again. | Tanzen wir noch einmal. |

tunts'-en vere noCH ine-mahl.

| It is very hot in here. | Es ist sehr warm hier. |

ez ist zair varm here.

| Let us sit down. | Setzen wir uns. |

zets'-en vere ŏŏns.

| May I see you home ? | Darf ich Sie nach Hause begleiten ? |

darf ich zee naCH how'-zer beg-lï'-ten.

| When shall I see you again ? | Wann sehe ich Sie wieder ? |

vun zay'-er ich zee vee'-der.

| Act, Scene. | Akt, Auftritt. |

uckt, owf'-tritt.

| Actor, Actress. | Schauspieler, Schau-spielerin. |

sh-ow'-shpeel-er, sh-ow'-shpeel-er-in.

| Comedy, Concert. | Lustspiel, Konzert. |

lŏŏst'-shpeel, kon-tsairt'.

| Documentary film, Drama. | Kulturfilm, Drama. |

kŏŏl-toor'-feelm, drah'-mah.

| Newsreel. | Wochenschau. |

voCH'-en-sh-ow.

Performance, Play.	Ausstellung, Schauspiel.

owce'-shtell-ŏŏng, sh-ow'-shpeel.

Principal part.	Hauptrolle.

howpt'-rol-ler.

Screen, Stage.	Leinwand, Bühne.

line'-vunt, bü'-ner.

Tragedy.	Tragödie.

tra-gurd'-ee-er.

RADIO

Is there a wireless in the hotel ?	Ist ein Radioapparat im Hotel ?

ist ine rahd'-io-up-ar-aht' im ho-tell'.

Switch on the wireless.	Stellen Sie das Radio an.

shtell'-en zee duss rahd'-io un.

Which knob do I turn ?	Welchen Knopf muss ich drehen ?

velch'-en knopf mŏŏss ich dray -en.

Tune in to London.	Schalten Sie London ein.

shult'-en zee lon'-don ine.

I want to hear the news.	Ich möchte die Nachrichten hören.

ich murch'-ter dee naCH'-richt-en hur'-ren.

The weather forecast comes first, then the news.	Der Wetterbericht kommt zuerst, dann die Nachrichten.

dair vet'-er-ber-icht kommt tsoo-airst', dun dee naCH'-richt-en.

The programme is finished.	Das Programm ist beendet.

duss pro-grum' ist bay-end'-et.

Turn to another station.	Schalten Sie einen andern Sender ein.

shult'-en zee i'-nen un'-dern zend'-er ine.

Do you want to hear dance-music ?	Möchten Sie Tanzmusik hören ?

murch'-ten zee tunts'-moo-zeek' hur'-ren.

It is coming through badly.	Wir empfangen es schlecht.

vere emp-fang'-en ez shlecht.

There is too much interference; you can hardly hear it.	Es ist zu viel Störung; man kann es kaum hören.

ez ist tsoo feel shtur'-roong ; mun kun ez kowm hur'ren.

Switch it off.	Stellen Sie es ab.

shtell'-en zee ez up.

Long-wave, medium-wave, short-wave.	Langwelle, Mittelwelle, Kurzwelle.

lung'-vell-er, mitt'-el-vell-er, kŏŏrts'-vell-er.

Aerial, Earth.	Antenne, Erdung.

un-ten'-er, aird'-ŏong.

SPORT

Are you keen on sport ?	Treiben Sie Sport ?

trī'-ben zee shport.

He is a great sportsman.	Er ist ein grosser Sportler.

air ist ine grŏss'-er shport'-ler.

Do you play tennis, golf ?	Spielen Sie Tennis, Golf ?

shpeel'-en zee ten'-iss, golf.

I should like a game with you.	Ich möchte gern mit Ihnen spielen.

ich murch'-ter gairn mit ee'-nen shpeel'-en.

Have you brought your tennis-racket, golf-clubs ?	Haben Sie Ihren Tennis-Schläger, Ihre Golf-Schläger, mitge-bracht.

hah'-ben zee ee'-ren ten'-iss-shlay-ger, ee'-rer golf'-shlay-ger mit'-geb-raCHt.

| Is there a tennis-court near ? | Gibt es einen Tennis-platz in der Nähe ? |

geebt ez ī'-nen ten'-iss-pluts in dair nay'-er.

| The tennis-courts are in front of the hotel. | Die Tennisplätze liegen vor dem Hotel. |

dee ten'-iss-plets-er lee'-gen fore dame ho-tell'.

| I have only three balls. | Ich habe nur drei Bälle. |

ich hah'-ber noor dry bell'-er.

| We have lost one ball. | Wir haben einen Ball verloren. |

vere hah'-ben ī'-nen bul fair-lo'-ren.

| We can have a good game here. | Hier können wir gut spielen. |

here kurn'-en vere goot shpeel'-en.

| You are much better than I. | Sie spielen viel besser als ich. |

zee shpeel'-en feel bess'-er uls ich.

| I should like to see a football match. | Ich möchte ein Fussball-spiel sehen. |

ich murch'-ter ine fooss'-bal-shpeel zay'-en.

| The first team. | Die erste Mannschaft. |

dee airst'-er mun'-shaft.

| Which is the way to the stadium ? | Wie komme ich zum Stadion ? |

vee komm'-er ich tsoŏm shtah'-dee-ōn.

| Two tickets for the stand, please. | Zwei Tribünenplätze, bitte. |

tsvī tree-bü'-nen-plets-er bitt'-er.

| Was it a goal ? | War das ein Tor ? |

var duss ine tore.

| Who won ? | Wer hat gewonnen ? |

vair hut gev-onn'-en.

| It was a draw. | Das Spiel war unent-schieden. |

duss shpeel var oŏn'-ent-shee-den.

Referee, Result.	Schiedsrichter, Ergebnis.

sheets'-rich-ter, er-gape'-nis.

| Let us go to the races. | Gehen wir zum Pferde-rennen. |

gay'-en vere tsoom pfair'-der-ren-nen.

| I should like to go to the —— to-morrow. | Ich möchte morgen zum —— gehen. |

ich murch'-ter mor'-gen tsoom —— gay'-en.

| Race-course, Race-horse. | Rennbahn, Rennpferd. |

renn'-bahn, renn'-pfairt.

| Race, Steeplechase. | Wettrennen, Wettrenn-en mit Hindernissen. |

vet'-renn-en, vet'-renn-en mit hin'-der-niss-en.

| Bet, Winning-post. | Wette, Ziel. |

vet'-er, tseel.

| Bicycle, Cyclist. | Fahrrad, Radfahrer. |

far'-raht, raht'-far-er.

| Is there riding, swim-ming here ? | Kann man hier reiten, schwimmen ? |

kun mun here rī'-ten, shvim'-en.

| Where is the bathing-place, swimming-pond ? | Wo ist die Badeanstalt, das Schwimmbad ? |

vo ist dee bahd'-er-un-shtult, duss shvim'-baht.

| Can I have a cubicle ? | Ich möchte eine Kabine haben. |

ich murch'-ter ī'-ner ka-bee'-ner hah'-ben.

| Give me a weekly ticket. | Geben Sie mir eine Wochenkarte. |

gay'-ben zee mere ī'-ner voCH'-en-kart-er.

| Bathing cap, costume. | Bademütze, Badeanzug. |

bah'-der-müt-ser, bah'-der-un-tsoog.

| Where can I hire a row-ing-boat ? | Wo kann ich ein Ruder-boot mieten ? |

vo kun ich ine roo'-der-boat mee'-ten.

I should like to hire a sailing-boat for this afternoon.	Ich möchte für heute nachmittag ein Segelboot mieten.

ich murch'-ter für hoy'-ter naCH'-mit-ahg ine zay'-gel-boat mee'-ten.

Do you have to be a member of the Yacht Club?	Muss man ein Mitglied vom Yachtklub sein?

mŏŏss mun ine mit'-gleed fom yaCH'-t-kloob zine.

Do you skate, ski?	Laufen Sie Schlittschuh, Ski?

lowf'-en zee shlitt'-shoo, shee.

I do not ski very well.	Ich laufe nicht sehr gut Ski.

ich lowf'-er nicht zair goot shee.

Ice-rink, ski slopes.	Eisbahn, Ski-Gelände.

ice'-bahn, shee'-gel-end-er.

Ski-boots, costume.	Skistiefel, Skianzug.

shee'-shteef-el, shee'-un-tsoog.

The skis are in the luggage-van.	Die Skier sind im Gepäckwagen.

dee shee'-er zint im gep-eck'-vahg-en.

Tournament, World champion.	Turnier, Weltmeister.

toor-neer', velt'-mī-ster.

Men's singles, women's singles.	Herreneinzel, Dameneinzel.

hair'-en-ine-tsel, dah'-men-ine-tsel.

Men's doubles, women's doubles.	Herrendoppel, Damendoppel.

hair'-en-dopp-el, dah'-men-dopp-el.

MOTORING

*Information on taking a car abroad should be obtained from
either the Automobile Association or the Royal Automobile Club,
who can provide the necessary papers and arrange for customs
facilities. Throughout Germany, Austria and Switzerland cars
drive on the right side of the road. Petrol is sold by the litre (liter,
pronounced leet'-er); one gallon equals about 4½ litres. Distances
and speed are measured in kilometres (kilometre— keel'-o-may-ter).
Current regulations regarding speed limit, lighting up times and so
on should be ascertained at the start of the journey.*

I want some petrol.	Ich möchte Benzin haben.
ich murch'-ter ben-tseen' hah'-ben.	
Give me —— litres, please.	Geben Sie mir bitte —— Liter.
gay'-ben zee mere bitt'-er —— leet'-er.	
Please see if I need oil.	Bitte, sehen Sie nach ob ich Öl brauche.
bitt'-er, zay'-en zee naCH op ich url browCH'-er.	
I need some oil too.	Ich brauche auch Öl.
ich browCH'-er owCH url.	
I need some more water in the radiator.	Ich brauche noch etwas Wasser im Kühler.
ich browCH'-er noCH et'-vuss vuss'-er im kü'-ler.	
That will do.	Es ist gut so.
ez ist goot zo.	
I need air in the tyres.	Ich brauche Luft in den Reifen.
ich browCH'-er looft in dane rī'-fen.	
I want to garage my car for a night, a week.	Ich möchte meinen Wagen für eine Nacht (acht Tage) einstellen.
ich murch'-ter mī'-nen vahg-en für ī'-ner naCHt (aCHt tahg'-er) ine'-shtell-en.	

It will be better if I reverse into the garage.	Es wird wohl besser sein, wenn ich rückwärts in die Garage hineinfahre.

ez virt vole bess′-er zine, ven ich rük′-vairts in dee gar-age′
(as in French) hin-ine′-far-er.

Give the car a wash and a greasing.	Waschen Sie und schmieren Sie den Wagen.

vush′-en zee ŏont shmeer′-en zee dane vahg′-en.

I have a puncture.	Ich habe eine Panne.

ich hah′-ber i′-ner punn′-er.

Can you mend it ?	Können Sie es reparieren ?

kurn′-en zee ez ray-par-eer′-en.

How long will it take ?	Wie lange wird es dauern ?

vee lung′-er virt ez dow′-ern.

Then I shall leave the car here.	Dann lasse ich das Auto hier.

dun luss′-er ich duss ow′-to here.

When can I collect it ?	Wann darf ich es abholen ?

vun darf ich ez up′-ho-len.

I'll be back in the afternoon.	Ich komme am Nachmittag wieder.

ich komm′-er um naCH′-mit-ahg vee′-der.

Where is the nearest garage for repairs ?	Wo ist die nächste Reparatur-Werkstätte ?

vo ist dee next′-er ray-par-a-toor′-vairk-shtett-er.

Can you tow me there ?	Können Sie mich dahin schleppen ?

kurn′-en zee mich dah-hin′ shlepp′-en.

| I have engine trouble. | Ich habe einen Motor-
defekt. |

ich hah'-ber ī'-nen mo-tōr'-day-fect.

| Please see what is wrong. | Bitte sehen Sie nach was
es ist. |

bitt'-er zay'-en zee naCH vuss ez ist.

| Is it serious ? | Ist es schlimm ? |

ist ez shlim.

| Please overhaul the
engine. | Bitte überholen Sie den
Motor. |

bitt'-er ü-ber-ho'-len zee dane mo-tōr'.

| The engine is overheated. | Der Motor ist überhitzt. |

dair mo-tōr' ist ü-ber-hitst'.

| It will not start. | Der Motor springt
nicht an. |

dair mo-tōr' shpringt nicht un.

| I have had a short-cir-
cuit. | Ich habe einen Kurz-
schluss gehabt. |

ich hah'-ber ī'-nen koorts'-shoo, German ger-hubt.

| One of my plugs is not
sparking. | Eine meiner Zündkerzen
arbeitet nicht. |

ī'-ner mīner tsünt'-kair-tsen ar'-bī-tet nicht.

| The brakes want adjust-
ing. | Die Bremsen müssen
angezogen werden. |

dee brem'-zen müss'-en un'-get-so-gen vaird'-en.

| The steering is loose. | Das Steuer ist locker. |

duss shtoy'-er ist lock'-er.

| Get into second, third
gear. | Schalten Sie den zweiten
(dritten) Gang ein. |

shult'-en zee dane tsvī'-ten (dritt'-en) gung ine.

| It is getting dark ; put
on the lights. | Es wird dunkel ; zünden
Sie die Lampen an. |

ez virt doonk'-el ; tsün'-den zee dee lump'-en un.

| The bridge is a long way from here. | Die Brücke ist sehr weit von hier. |

dee brük'-er ist zair vite fon here.

| Is there a car-ferry ? | Gibt es eine Autofähre ? |

geebt ez i'-ner ow'-to-fair-er.

| Can you point me out the route on the map ? | Können Sie mir den Weg auf der Karte zeigen ? |

kurn'-en zee mere dane vaig owf dair kart'-er tsī'-gen.

| I am a stranger here. | Ich bin fremd hier. |

ich bin fremt here.

| I did not know that it was a one-way street. | Ich wusste nicht, dass es eine Einbahnstrasse ist. |

ich vōoss'-ter nicht duss ez i'-ner ine'-bahn-shtrahss-er ist.

| I did not see the traffic lights (road sign). | Ich habe die Verkehrsampel (das Verkehrszeichen) nicht gesehen |

ich hah'-ber dee fair-kairz-ump'-el (duss fair-kairz'-tsī-chen) nicht gez-ay'-en.

| Here is my driving licence. | Hier ist mein Führerschein. |

here ist mine für'-er-shine.

| I have had an accident. | Ich habe einen Unfall gehabt. |

ich hah'-ber-i'-nen ōon'-ful ger-hubt'.

| I forgot to keep to the right. | Ich vergass, rechts zu fahren. |

ich fair-gahss', rechts tsoo far'-en.

| The car skidded. | Das Auto hat gerutscht. |

duss ow'-to hut ger-ōōtsht.

| The lorry overtook me on the bend. | Der Lastwagen hat mich an der Kurve überholt. |

dair lust'-vahg-en hut mich un dair koor'-ver ü-ber-hōlt'.

| He did not see the cyclist. | Er hat den Radfahrer nicht gesehen. |

air hut dane raht'-far-er ni*ch*t gez-ay'-en.

| He was driving too quickly. | Er fuhr zu schnell. |

air foor tsoo shnell.

| Maximum speed. | Höchstgeschwindigkeit. |

hu*r*kst'-gesh-vin-di*ch*-kite.

| Accelerator, Brake. | Gas, Bremse. |

gus, brem'-zer.

| Battery, Carburettor. | Akkumulator, Vergaser. |

a-koo-moo-laht'-or, fair-gahz'-er.

| Chains, Clutch. | Ketten, Kupplung. |

kett'-en, ko͞op'-lo͞ong.

| Cyclist, Garage. | Radfahrer, Garage. |

raht'-far-er, gar-age' (as French).

| Gear, Gear-box. | Gang, Getriebekasten. |

gung, ger-treeb'-er-kust-en.

| Gear-lever, Headlight. | Schalthebel, Scheinwerfer. |

shult'-hay-bel, shine'-ver-fer.

| Horn, Inner tube. | Hupe, Schlauch. |

hoop'-e*r*, shlowCH.

| Jack, Magneto. | Wagenheber, Magnet. |

vahg'-en-hay-ber, mug-nate'.

| Motor-bike, Mudguard. | Motorrad, Schutzblech. |

mo-tōr'-raht, sho͞ots'-ble*ch*.

| Oil, Parking-place. | Öl, Parkplatz. |

u*r*l, park'-pluts.

| Pedestrian, Petrol. | Fussgänger, Benzin. |

fooss'-geng-er, ben'-tseen'.

| Petrol station, Petrol tank. | Tankstelle, Benzintank. |

tunk'-shtell-e*r*, ben-tseen'-tunk.

Rear-light, Reverse gear.	Rücklampe, Rückwärts-gang.

rük'-lump-er, rük'-vairts-gung.

Sidelight, Sign-post.	Seitenlampe, Wegweiser.

zi'-ten-lump-er, vaig'-vi-zer.

Sparking-plug, Starter.	Zündkerze, Anlasser.

tsünt'-kairts—er, un'-luss-er.

Traffic policeman, Tyre.	Verkehrspolizist, Reifen.

fair-kairz'-pol-it-sist, ri'-fen.

Wheel, Windscreen.	Rad, Scheibe.

raht, shi'-ber.

Windscreen wiper.	Scheibenwischer.

shi'-ben-vish-er.

COUNTRIES AND NATIONALITIES

Before the last war, the meaning of Britain and British was hardly known to Germans; even now, they almost always speak of England, English, when they mean Britain.

Great Britain.	Grossbritannien.

grōss-britt-un'-ee-en.

England, English, an Englishman.	England, englisch, ein Engländer.

eng'-lunt, eng'-lish, ine eng'-lend-er.

Scotland, Scottish, a Scotsman.	Schottland, schottisch, ein Schotte.

shot'-lunt, shot'-tish, ine shot'-ter.

Ireland, Irish, an Irish-man.	Irland, irisch, ein Ire.

eer'-lunt, eer'-ish, ine eer'-er.

Wales, Welsh, a Welsh-man.	Wales, waliser, ein Waliser.

wales, val-eez'-er, ine val-eez'-er.

Europe, European, a European.	Europa, europäisch, ein Europäer.
oy-rope'-a, oy-ro-pay'-ish, ine oy-ro-pay'-er.	
Africa, African, an African.	Afrika, afrikanisch, ein Afrikaner.
uf'-rik-a, uf-rik-ahn'-ish, ine uf-rik-ahn'-er.	
Asia, Asiatic, an Asiatic.	Asien, asiatisch, ein Asiat.
ah'-zee-en, ah-zee-aht'-ish, ine ah-zee-aht'.	
Australia, Australian, an Australian.	Australien, australisch, ein Australier.
ows-trahl'-ee-en, ows-trahl'-ish, ine ows-trahl'-ee-er.	
Canada, Canadian, a Canadian.	Kanada, kanadisch, ein Kanadier.
kun'-ah-dah, kun-ahd'-ish, ine kun-ahd'-ee-er.	
America, American, an American.	Amerika, amerikanisch, ein Amerikaner.
um-air'-ee-ka, um-air-ee-kah'-nish, ine um-air-ee-kah'-ner.	
Austria, Austrian, an Austrian.	Österreich, österreichisch, ein Österreicher.
urst'-er-rĭch, urst'-er-rich-ish, ine urst'-er-rĭch-er.	
Belgium, Belgian, a Belgian.	Belgien, belgisch, ein Belgier.
belg'-ee-en, belg'-ish, ine belg'-ee-er.	
Czechoslovakia, Czechoslovakian, a Czech.	Die Tschechoslowakei, tschechisch, ein Tscheche.
dee chech-o-slo-vah-kī', chech'-ish, ine chech'-er.	
Denmark, Danish, a Dane.	Dänemark, dänisch, ein Däne.
dane'-er-mark, dane'-ish, ine dane'-er.	
France, French, a Frenchman.	Frankreich, französisch, ein Franzose.
frunk'-rĭch, frun-tsur'-zish, ine frun-tso'-zer.	

Finland, Finnish, a Finn.	Finnland, finnisch, ein Finnländer.

fin'-lunt, fin'-ish, ine fin'-lend-er.

Germany, German, a German.	Deutschland, deutsch, ein Deutscher.

doytsh'-lunt, doytsh, ine doytsh'-er.

Greece, Greek, a Greek.	Griechenland, griech-isch, ein Grieche.

greech'-en-lunt, greech'-ish, ine greech'-er.

Holland, Dutch, a Dutchman.	Holland, holländisch, ein Holländer.

holl'-unt, holl-end'-ish, ine holl-end'-er.

Hungary, Hungarian, a Hungarian.	Ungarn, ungarisch, ein Ungar.

ŏŏng'-garn, ŏŏng-gar'-ish, ine ŏŏng'-gar.

Italy, Italian, an Italian.	Italien, italienisch, ein Italiener.

it-ahl'-ee-en, it-ahl-ee-ain'-ish, ine it-ahl-ee-ain'-er.

Norway, Norwegian, a Norwegian.	Norwegen, norwegisch, ein Norweger.

nor'-vay-gen, nor-vay'-gish, ine nor-vay'-ger.

Poland, Polish, a Pole.	Polen, polnisch, ein Pole.

pole'-en, pol'-nish, ine pole'-er.

Portugal, Portuguese, a Portuguese.	Portugal, portugiesisch, ein Portugiese.

por'-too-gal, por-too-gee'-zish, ine por-too-gee'-zer.

Russia, Russian, a Russian.	Russland, russisch, ein Russe.

rŏŏss'-land, rŏŏss'-ish, ine rŏŏss'-er.

Spain, Spanish, a Spaniard.	Spanien, spanisch, ein Spanier.

shpah'-nee-en, shpah'-nish, ine shpah'-nee-er.

Sweden, Swedish, a Swede.	Schweden, schwedisch, ein Schwede.

shvay'-den, shvay'-dish, ine shvay'-der.

Switzerland (in Switzerland), Swiss, a Swiss.	Die Schweiz (in der Schweiz), schweizerisch, ein Schweizer.

dee shvīts (in dare shvīts), shvīts'-er-ish ine, shvīts'-er.

North Sea, English Channel.	Nordsee, der Kanal.

nort'-zay, dair kun-ahl'.

Berlin, Cologne, Munich.	Berlin, Köln, München.

bair-leen', kurin, mün'-chen.

Brussels, Paris, Vienna.	Brüssel, Paris, Wien.

brü'-sel, par-eece', veen.

Basle, Geneva.	Basel, Genf.

bah'-zel, genf.

Rome, Florence, Milan.	Rom, Florenz, Mailand.

rome, flōr-ents', mī'-lunt.

Naples, Venice.	Neapel, Venedig.

nay-ah'-pel, ven-ay'-dich.

Flushing, Hook of Holland.	Vlissingen, Hoek van Holland.

fliss'-ing-en, hōōk van holl'-unt.

NUMERALS

1	**Eins.**	17	**Siebzehn.**
	ïnce.		zeep'-tsain.
2	**Zwei.**	18	**Achtzehn.**
	tsvï.		aCHt'-tsain.
3	**Drei.**	19	**Neunzehn.**
	dry.		noyn'-tsain.
4	**Vier.**	20	**Zwanzig.**
	fear.		tsvun'-tsich.
5	**Fünf.**	21	**Einundzwanzig.**
	fünf.		ïne'-ŏŏnt-tsvun'-tsich.
6	**Sechs.**	30	**Dreissig.**
	zex.		dry'-sich.
7	**Sieben.**	40	**Vierzig.**
	zee'-ben.		fear'-tsich.
8	**Acht.**	50	**Fünfzig.**
	aCHt.		fünf'-tsich.
9	**Neun.**	60	**Sechzig.**
	noyn.		zech'-tsich.
10	**Zehn.**	70	**Siebzig.**
	tsain.		zeep'-tsich.
11	**Elf.**	80	**Achtzig.**
	elf.		aCHt'-tsich.
12	**Zwölf.**	90	**Neunzig.**
	tsvurlf.		noyn'-tsich.
13	**Dreizehn.**	100	**Hundert.**
	dry'-tsain.		hŏŏn'-dert.
14	**Vierzehn.**	200	**Zweihundert.**
	fear'-tsain.		tsvï-hŏŏn'-dert.
15	**Fünfzehn.**	1000	**Tausend.**
	fünf'-tsain.		tow'-zent.
16	**Sechzehn.**	2000	**Zwei-tausend.**
	zech'-tsain.		tsvï tow'-zent.

A hundred thousand. | Hundert tausend.
hŏŏn'-dert tow'-zent.

A million. | Eine Million.
ĭ'-ner mill-i-ōn'.

First.	Erste.	Fourth.	Vierte.
airst'-er.		fear'-ter.	

Second.	Zweite.	Fifth.	Fünfte.
tsvī'-ter.		fünf'-ter.	

Third.	Dritte.	Tenth.	Zehnte.
dritt'-er.		tsain'-ter.	

Twentieth. | Zwanzigste.
tsvun'-tsich-ster.

Twenty-first. | Einundzwanzigste.
ine-ōont-tsvun'-tsich-ster.

Fiftieth. | Fünfzigste.
fünf'-tsich-ster.

Hundredth. | Hundertste.
hŏŏn'-dert-ster.

Half, a third. | Halb, Ein Drittel.
hulp, ine dritt'-el.

A quarter, A fifth. | Ein Viertel, ein Fünftel.
ine fear'-tel, ine fünf'-tel.

1950. | Neunzehnhundertfünf-
zig.
noyn'-tsain-hŏŏn-dert-fünf'-tsich.

1789. | Siebzehnhundertneun-
undachtzig.
zeep'-tsain-hŏŏn-dert-noyn-ōont-aCHt'-sich.

Page 63. | Seite dreiundsechzig.
zī'-ter dry'-ōont-zech'-tsich.

Number 426. | Nummer vierhundert-
sechsundzwanzig.
nŏŏm'-er fear'-hŏŏn-dert-zex-ōont-tsvun'-tsich.

LIQUID MEASURE		AREA		PRESSURE	
Litres	*Pints*	*Hectares*	*Acres*	*Pounds per sq. inch*	*Kilograms per sq. centimetre*
0·284	0·5	·40	1	20	1·406
0·5	0·88	1	2·47	21	1·476
0·57	1	2	4·94	22	1·547
1	1·76	3	7·41	23	1·617
2	3·52	4	9·88	24	1·687
3	5·28	5	12·36	25	1·758
4	7·04	6	14·83	26	1·828
5	8·80	7	17·30	27	1·898
	*Gallons**	8	19·77	28	1·969
6	1·32	9	22·24	29	2·039
7	1·54	10	24·71	30	2·109
8	1·76	15	37·07	31	2·180
9	1·98	20	49·42	32	2·250
10	2·20	25	61·78	33	2·320
15	3·3	35	86·49	34	2·390
20	4·40	45	111·20	35	2·461
25	5·50	55	135·91	36	2·531
35	7·70	65	160·62	37	2·601
45	9·90	75	185·34	38	2·671
50	11·00	85	210·05	39	2·742

*British Imperial gallons, 1 of which equals 1·2 U.S. gallons.

DAYS OF THE WEEK

Sunday, Monday. | Sonntag, Montag.
zonn'-tahg, moan'-tahg.

Tuesday, Wednesday. | Dienstag, Mittwoch.
deenst'-ahg, mitt'-voCH.

Thursday, Friday. | Donnerstag, Freitag.
donn'-ers-tahg, fry'-tahg.

Saturday. | Samstag, or Sonnabend.
zums'-tahg, zonn-ah'-bent.

MONTHS

January, February.	Januar, Februar.
	yan'-oo-ar, faib'-roo-ar.
March, April.	März, April.
	mairts, up-ril'.
May, June.	Mai, Juni.
	my, yoon'-ee.
July, August.	Juli, August.
	yool'-ee, ow-gōōst'.
September, October.	September, Oktober.
	zep-tem'-ber, oc-tō'-ber.
November, December.	November, Dezember.
	no-vem'-ber, day-tsem'-ber.

TIME—GENERAL PHRASES

A day, month.	Ein Tag, Monat.
	ine tahg, mō'-naht.
A week.	Eine Woche, Acht Tage.
	i'-ner voCH'-er, aCHt tahg'-er.
A fortnight.	Vierzehn Tage.
	fear'-tsain tahg'-er.
Three months.	Drei Monate.
	dry mō'-naht-er.
A year, two years.	Ein Jahr, zwei Jahre.
	ine yar, tsvī yar'-er.
To-day, yesterday.	Heute, Gestern.
	hoy'-ter, guess'-tern.
Day before yesterday.	Vorgestern.
	fore'-guess-tern.
Yesterday evening.	Gestern abend.
	guess'-tern ah'-bent.
To-morrow.	Morgen.
	morg'-en.

To-morrow morning. | Morgen früh.

morg'-en frü.

Day after to-morrow. | Übermorgen.

ü'-ber-morg-en.

A month ago. | Vor einem Monat.

fore ī'-nem mō'-naht.

For some days past. | Seit einigen Tagen.

zite ī'-nig-en tahg'-en.

Every day, daily. | Jeden Tag, täglich.

yay'-den tahg, tay'-glich.

TIME—THE CLOCK

What time is it ? | Wie spät ist es ?

vee shpate ist ez.

It is one o'clock. | Es ist ein Uhr.

ez ist ine oor.

10 o'clock. | Zehn Uhr.

tsain oor.

Quarter past 10. | Viertel nach zehn.

fear'-tel naCH tsain.

Half-past 10. | Halb elf (that is, " half before 11 ").

hulp elf.

Quarter to 11. | Viertel vor elf.

fear'-tel fore elf.

11 a.m. | Elf Uhr morgens.

elf oor morg'-enz.

11 p.m. | Elf Uhr abends.

elf oor ah'-bents.

Twenty past 6. | Zwanzig nach sechs.

tsvunts'-ich naCH zex.

Midday, Midnight. | Mittag, Mitternacht.

mitt'-ahg, mitt'-er-naCHt.

Morning, Afternoon. | Morgen, Nachmittag.

morg'-en, naCH'-mitt-ahg.

GERMAN-ENGLISH SECTION

PUBLIC NOTICES AND COMMON PHRASES

Abteil für Schwerbe-
schädigte.

Compartment reserved
for use of war-
disabled.

up'-tile für shvair'-besh-aid'-ich-ter.

Achtung !

Attention !

aCH'-toong.

Alle aussteigen (einsteigen,
umsteigen) !

All out (of train, etc.),
all aboard, all change !

ull'-er owce'-shtī-gen (ine'-shtī-gen, ōōm'-shtī-gen.

Auskunft (Büro).

Information (Office).

owce'-koonft.

Alle Fahrkarten bitte,
(In Switzerland, alle
Billets).

All tickets, please.

ull'-er far'-kart-en (ull'-er bee'-yay) bitt'-er.

Autobahn.

Trunk road, for fast
traffic.

ow'-to-bahn.

Bahnhofsvorsteher.

Station-master.

bahn'-hōfs-fore-shtay·er.

Besetzt.

Engaged (on doors).

ber-zetst'.

Äusserlich zu gebrauch-
en.

For external use only
(on medicine bottles).

oyss'-er-lich tsoo geb-rowCH'-en.

Damen (toilette).

Ladies (toilet).

dah'-men.

Das Betreten des Rasens
ist verboten.

Keep off the grass.

duss ber-tray'-ten dez rah'-zenz ist fair·boat'-en.

Das Sprechen mit dem Fahrer während der Fahrt ist verboten.	It is forbidden to speak to the driver during the journey.

duss shprech'-en mit dame far'-er vay'-rent dair fahrt ist fair-boat'-en.

Drücken.	Press, Push (on bells, doors, etc.).

drük'-en.

Durchgangszug.	Through train.

dŏŏrch'-gungz-tsoog.

Einbahnstrasse.	One-way street.

ine'-bahn-shtrahss-er.

Eintritt frei.	Admission free.

ine'-tritt fry.

Ersatz.	Substitute.

er-zuts'.

Familienname.	Surname.

fa-meei'-ee-en-nahm-er.

Fernsprecher.	Telephone.

fairn'-shprech-er.

Feuerwehr.	Fire Brigade.

foy'-er-vair.

Frei.	Free, Vacant.

fry.

Fundbüro.	Lost Property Office.

fŏŏnt'-bü-ro.

Genaue Adresse.	Precise address.

ger-now'-er a-dress'-er.

Gepäckbahnsteig. Nicht aussteigen.	Luggage platform. Do not alight.

ger-peck'-bahn-shtīg. nicht owce'-shti-gen.

Gift.	Poison.

gift.

Hauptbahnhof.	Main station.

howpt'-bahn-hofe.

Heben.	Lift, Raise.
hay'-ben.	
Herren.	Gentlemen.
hair'-en.	
Hinten einsteigen.	Enter at the rear (on trams, etc.).
hin'-ten ine'-shti-gen.	
Kalt (K.).	Cold.
kult.	
Kein Ausgang (Durch-gang, Eingang).	No exit (thoroughfare, entrance).
kine owce'-gung (dŏŏrch'-gung, ine'-gung).	
Klopfen.	Knock.
klopf'-en.	
Krankenhaus, Kranken-wagen.	Hospital, Ambulance.
krunk'-en-house, krunk'-en-vahg-en.	
Langsam fahren.	Drive slowly.
lung'-zum far'-en.	
Mit Zuschlag.	With supplementary charge.
mit tsoo'-shlahg.	
Nachmittags geschlossen.	Closed in the afternoon.
naCH'-mitt-ahgs ger-shloss'-en.	
Nicht hinauslehnen.	Do not lean out.
nicht hin-owce'-lay-nen.	
Nicht parken.	No parking.
nicht park'-en.	
Nicht rauchen (Raucher).	No smoking (non-smoker).
nicht rowCH'-en (rowCH'-er).	
Notausgang.	Emergency exit.
note'-owce-gung.	

Notbremse.	Communication cord, emergency brake.
note'-brem-zer.	
Parkplatz.	Parking-place.
park'-pluts.	
Personenzug.	Local train.
pair-zone'-en-tsoog.	
Polizei (amt).	Police (Office).
pol-its-ī' (umt).	
Postamt.	Post Office.
posst'-umt.	
Rauchen verboten.	No smoking.
rowCH'-en fair-boat'-en.	
Rauchen im Gang ist (nicht) gestattet.	Smoking in the corridor is (not) allowed.
rowCH'-en im gung ist (niCHt) gesh-tutt'-et.	
Raucherabteil.	Smoking compartment.
rowCH'-er-up'-tile.	
Reiseandenken.	Souvenir articles.
rī'-zer-un'-denk-en.	
Reisebüro.	Travel agency.
rī'-zer-bü-ro.	
Schellen.	Ring.
shell'-en.	
Schnellzug.	Express train.
shnell'-tsoog.	
Strengstens verboten.	Strictly forbidden.
shtreng'-stens fair-boat'en.	
Trinkwasser.	Drinking water.
trink'-vuss-er.	
Umleitung.	Diversion (of traffic, etc.).
o͝om'-lī-to͝ong.	
Unterschrift.	Signature.
o͝on'-ter-shrift.	

Verbotener Durchgang.	No thoroughfare.
fair-boat'-en-er dŏŏr<i>ch</i>'-gung.	
Vorname.	Christian name.
fore'-nahm-er.	
Vorn aussteigen.	Alight at the front (of vehicles).
fōrn owce'-shtī-gen.	
Warm (W.).	Hot.
varm.	
Wartesaal (erster, zweiter, dritter Klasse).	Waiting Room (1st, 2nd, 3rd class).
vart'-er-zahl (airst'-er, tsvī'-ter, dritt'-er kluss'-er).	
Ziehen.	Pull.
tsee'-en.	
Zollamt.	Customs.
tsoll'-umt.	

GERMAN ABBREVIATIONS

Abf., *Abfahrt*, Departure.

B.W., *Bitte wenden*, Please turn over.

A.Ch., *Ante Christo*, Before Christ.

a/M, *am Main*, e.g. *Frankfurt am Main*.

Ank., *Ankunft*, Arrival.

a/O, *an der Oder*, e.g. *Frankfurt an der Oder*.

a/Rh, *am Rhein*.

Bayr., *Bayrisch*, Bavarian.

Bez., *Bezirk*, District.

BP, *Beschleunigter Personenzug*, Fast train, but not non-stop.

CH. (Swiss), *Confederatio Helveticae*, used on cars, like " G.B."

D., *Deutschland*, Germany.

DM, *D Mark*, German Mark. The unit of the revised German currency.

DPf, *D. Pfennig*, One-hundredth part of the D Mark.

D-Zug, *Durchgangszug*, Through or corridor train.

Eidg. (Swiss), *Eidgenössisch*, Federal.

Fr., *Frau*, Mrs.

Frl., *Fräulein*, Miss.

geb., *geboren*, born.

Gebr., *Gebrüder*, Brothers.

HBF., *Hauptbahnhof*, Main station.

Hr., *Herr*, Mr.

i., *in*, " in " ; e.g. *Hagen i.W.*, Hagen in Westphalia.

i.P., *in Preussen*, in Prussia.

JH, *Jugendherberge*, Youth Hostel.

kg., *Kilogramm*, Kilogram.

km., *Kilometer*, Kilometre.

MEZ, *Mittel-europäische Zeit*, Central European Time (one hour ahead of Greenwich Mean Time).

möbl., *möbliert*, furnished.

Nachf., *Nachfolger*, Successor.

n.Chr, *Nach Christo*, After Christ, A.D.

N, *Norden*, North.

NO, *Nordosten*, North-East.

NW, *Nordwesten*, North-West.

O, *Osten*, East.

Ostpr., *Ostpreussen*, East Prussia.

p.A., *per Adresse*, Care of, C/o.

Pf., *Pfennig* (see DPf).

Pfd., *Pfund*, Pound.

PS, *Pferdestärke*, Horse power, h.p.

qm., *Quadratmeter*, Square metre.

Reg.Bez., *Regierungsbezirk*, Administrative district.

Rh., *Rhein*, Rhine.

röm.-kath., *römisch-katholisch*, Roman-Catholic.

Rp. (Swiss), *Rappen, centime* (one hundredth part of Swiss franc).

S., *Süden*, South.

SBB (Swiss), *Schweizer Bundesbahnen*, Swiss Federal Railways.

Skt., *Sankt*, Saint.

Str., *Strasse*, Street.

u., *und*, and.

u.A.w.g., *Um Antwort wird gebeten*, A reply is requested, R.S.V.P.

v., *von.*, of, from.

vorm., *vormals*, formerly ; *vormittags*, before noon, a.m.

W., *Westen*, West.

WEZ., *Westeuropäische Zeit*, Western European Time (Greenwich Mean Time).

W.S.g.u., *Wenden Sie gefälligst um.*, P.T.O.

z., *zu*, to.

z.B., *Zum Beispiel*, for example, e.g.

WORTVERZEICHNIS

*Die in grossen Buchstaben gedruckten Worte bezeichnen Kapitel, in
denen der Gegenstand ausführlich behandelt ist.*

Page	Page	Page
Abend 62, 137	Austern 112	Bilder, galerie 67, 69
Abendanzug 59, 91	Australien 131	Bildhauerei 69
Abendessen	Auto 128	Billig 54, 95
31, 55, 106, 110, 114	Autobus 46, 64, 116	Binde 83
Abführmittel 82	— haltestelle 64	Birne 112
Abkürzungen	AUTOFAHREN	Bitte 17, 107
144-145	13, 125-130	Blasen 81
Abschied 59-62, 75	Auto-Fähre 128	Bleistift 88
Abteil 29	Auto mieten 66	Blumenkohl 109
Adresse		Bluse 90
20, 63, 75, 103	Bad 53, 56	Blutwurst 108
Aermel (kurz,	Badeanzug 90, 123	Bohnen 108
lang) 94	Bademütze 90, 123	Botanischer
Aermelkanal 133	— salz 82	Garten 68
Afrika 131	— zimmer 55	Bote 58
Alpenstock 90	BAHNHOF, AM 32	Brandy 109
Amerika 131	Bahnhof	Bremse 127, 129
Ammoniak 81	26, 28, 61, 64, 65	Brennstoff 77
Ananas 112	Bahnhofspolizei 37	Briefe, absenden
ANKUNFT, DIE	— vorsteher 37	37, 38
26-27	Bahnsteig 28, 65	— nachfragen 58
Anmeldung,	— karte 30	— nachsenden 61
polizeilich 99	Ball 122	BRIEFE SCHREIBEN
Anzug 57	Band 97	24
Apfel 108	BANK DIE 89	
Apfelwein 109	Bar 44, 55	Briefmarken
APOTHEKE, DIE	Basel 133	36, 78, 93
80-84	Baumwolle 90	Brille 91, 96
Apotheke 101	Bein 101, 107	Brot 61, 109
Aprikosen 108	Belgien 131	Brötchen 105, 113
Arzt 82, 100, 101	Benzin 125, 129	Brücke 128
Asien 131	— tanken 125	Brüssel 133
Aufnahmen	Berg 70	Brust 107
machen 70	Berlin 133	BUCH & PAPIER-
Auf Wiedersehen	BESUCH, DER 73-75	HANDLUNG 87-88
18, 75	Bett 30, 53, 102	Bücher 35, 79, 87
AUSFLUG, DER	Bettdecke 56	Buffet 34
63-72	Bezirk 144	BÜRO, IM 58-59
Auskunft 10, 37	Bier 108	Bürste, Haar 91
Aussicht 70	Bilder 71	— Kleider 90
		— Nagel 83

146

Page

Bürste, Zahn 84
Butter 105, 109

Chauffeur 66
Cognac
    45, 48, 100, 109

Damen 37
Dampfer 43
— Abfahrt 43
— Ankunft 44
Danke 17, 72, 107
Dänemark 131
Deck 44
Decke 31, 35, 47
Denkmal 70
Deutsch 18, 74,
    87, 106, 117, 132
DEUTSCH-ENGLISCH
    (gebräuchliche
    Phrasen) 139-143
Deutschland 88, 132
Docht 77
Dom 68
Durchfall 80

Eier 108, 110
Eile 21, 33, 35, 52
Einbahnstrasse 128
EINKAUFE 76-89
— WORTLISTE 90-93
Einladung 74
Einschreiben,
    Briefe 78
— Gepäck 32
Eintritt 69
Eis 111
Eis-Stadion 124
Ende 79
England 75, 130
Englisch
    18, 63, 66, 76, 80,
    87, 100, 117, 130
Ente 110
Entschuldigen,
    sich 17
Erbsen 112
— Suppe 112
Erdbeeren 114
Erkältung 80, 102

Page

Ersatzblei 88
Essen 43, 71, 118
Essig 115
Etikett 61
Europa 131

Fahrkarten 30, 43
FAHRPLAN 38
Fahrrad 123
Fahrstuhl 53
Familie 73
Farben 94
Farbfilm 86
Federhalter 88
Fenster
    21, 40, 48, 55, 106
Feuer 40, 55
Feuerstein 77
Feuerzeug 77
Film (Kamera)
    86, 98
— (Kino) 117
Fisch 110
Flanell 82
Flasche 88, 115
— (Wärm—) 56
Fleisch, gebraten
    108
— gekocht 108
— kalt 110
Florenz 133
Flugplatz 46
Flugpost 78
Flugzeug 46
Fluss 47, 70
Föhn 86
Fragen, einfache
    19, 22-23
Frankreich 131
Frau 73
Freunde, nach-
    fragen 73
FRISEUR, BEIM 84-86
Frühstück 31, 105
Führer 67, 69, 72
— (Buch) 63
— Schein 128
Fundbüro 37
Fussball 122
Füsse 81

Page

Gabel 107, 110
Garage 126, 129
Garn 91
Gas 129
Geflügel 113
GELD 14
— abheben 89
— deutsch 14, 49
— österr 14
— schweizer 13
Gemüse 115
Genf 133
GEPACK 32
— aufgeben 32
— Handgepäck 34
— Kontrolle 49-52
— schalter 32
— schein 33
— tragen 32
— träger 32
— versichern 33
— wagen 32, 124
Geschäftsviertel 53
Gestern 137
GEWICHTE &
    MASSE 136
Glas 96, 102, 115
Golf spielen 121
Grenze 26
Grüsse 24
Gurgeln 82
Gürtel 90
Guten Abend 17
— Morgen 17
— Tag 17

Haarklemme 86
— netz 86
— schneiden 84
Halle 106
Halsschmerzen 102
Hammel 112
Hand 81, 101
— gelenk 101
— gepäck 34
— koffer 35, 93
Handschuhe 91, 94
Handtuch 56, 84, 93
Hände waschen 22
Hauptstädte 133

	Page
Hecht	111
Heiss	41, 71, 86, 119
Heizung	41
Hemd	62, 91, 92
Heufieber	80
Heute	71, 137
— abend	62, 78, 98
Höchstgesch-	
windigkeit	129
Holland	132
Honig	105
Hook von	
Holland	133
Hose	93
Hotel	52
HOTEL, IM	55-57
Huhn	109
Hühnerauge	81
Hummer	111
Hupe	129
Hut	91
Influenza	102
Inserat	99
Irland	130
Italien	132
Ja	17, 107
Jahr	137
Jod	102
Kabine	43, 44, 123
Kaffee	105, 109
Kamm	82
Kalbfleisch	115
Kalbskopf	109
Kalt	41, 107
Kame.a	90
— reparieren	97
Kanada	131
Kaninchen	113
Karotten	109
Kartenspiel	88
— Besuchs	73
Kartoffeln	113
Katalog	71
Kaviar	109
Käse	109
Kellner	41
Ketten	129

	Page
Kino	118
Kirche	67
Kissen	31
Klassen (Zug)	29, 30
Kleid	91
Kleiderbürste	90
— bürsten	57
— stopfen	63
Kleidungsstücke	
	90-93
Kleingeld	60, 117
Klinge (Rasier)	83
Klingel	41
Klinik	82
Knöchel	101
Koffer	51
— reparieren	98
Köln	30, 133
Konsulat (Brit.)	23
Kopf	101
— schmerzen	
	81, 102
— tuch	91
— waschen	84
Kraftwagen	128
Kragen	62, 90
Krankenhaus	82
— schwester	102
Krankenwagen	100
KRANKHEITEN	
	100-102
Krawatte	93
— weisse	91
Kreditbrief	49, 89
Kuchen	109
Kühler	125
Kupplung	129
Kürbis	115
Kurzschluss	127
Laken	56
Lamm	111
Landen	43, 46, 47
Landkarte	
	63, 88, 128
LÄNDER &	
VÖLKER	130-133
Lauch	111
Leber	111
Leder	87

	Page
Licht	41, 127
Lied	119
Liegestuhl	44
Likör	111
Limonade	111
Links	65
Linse	96
Lippenstift	82, 91
Liter	125, 136
Locke	85
Lockenwickel	86
Löffel	107, 114
Luftkrankheit	48
Luftpost	78
Luftverkehr, s.	
REISEN	
Magenpulver	83
— schmerzen	81
Magnet	129
Mailand	133
Mann	73
Manschetten-	
knopf	91
Mantel	35, 90
Marmelade	105, 111
Massage,	
Gesichts	85
MASSE &	
GEWICHTE	136
Medizinen, s.	
APOTHEKE	
Melone	112
Messer	107, 111
Milch	112
— pulver	110
Mittag	138
Mitte	85
Mitternacht	138
Monat	138
MONATE, DIE	137
Morgen	72, 138
Motor	127
Museum	67
Musik	92
Mückenstiche	81
München	133
Nacht	125
— hemd	92

	Page
Nachtisch	110
Nagel (Finger)	85
— feile	83
— lack	83
— lackentferner	83
Name	73, 80
Neapel	133
Neffe	73
Nein	17
Nerv	103
Nichtraucher	29, 40
Nichte	73
Niere	111
Nordsee	133
Norwegen	132
Notbremse	42
Nummer	54, 58, 135
NUMMER	134-135
Oberkellner	107
Obst	110
Oel, Rizinus	82
— Haar	82, 85
— Salat	112
— Schmier	125, 129
— Sonnenbrand	83
Oelsardinen	113
Oelseide	83
Oesterreich	
	13, 14, 131
Ohrenschmerzen	81
Oliven	112
Omelette	112
Onkel	73
Oper	58
Opernglas	117
Orangen	112
Orchester	117
Paket	35, 78
PAPIERGESCHAFT	
	87-88
Paris	133
Park	68
Parkplatz	129
Pass	45, 49
— Ratschläge	9
— revision	45, 49
Pause	117
Pension	54

	Page
Pfeffer	112
Pfeife	77
Pfeifenreiniger	77
Pferderennen	123
Pfirsich	112
Pflaume	113
Pfund	136
PHOTOGRAPHIE	86
Pillen	83
Pilze	112
Plätze (Zug)	29, 30
Plombieren	103
Polen	132
POLIZEI	99
Polizist	100
Portier	59
POSTAMT, DAS	78-80
Postanweisunk	79
Postkarte	38, 78
Postlagernd	79
Preis	30
Programm	117
— (Rundfunk)	120
Pudding	110
Puger	83, 92
Pullover	92
Punkte	107
Pyjama	92
Quinin	83
Quittung	60
Radfahrer	123, 129
RADIO	120-121
Rasierklinge	83
— pinsel	83
Rathaus	68
RATSCHLÄGE,	
ALLGEMEINE	13
Rauchen	118
Raucher	29
Rechnung (wie	
man bezahlt)	
	59, 108
Rechts	65
Reifen (Auto)	
	125, 130
— schaden	126
Reis	113
Reise	26

	Page
Reiseandenken	93
— decke	93
— scheck	49, 59, 89
REISEN	
— Allgemeines	9-11
— Bahn	26-42
— Luft	9, 46-49
— See	9, 43-45
— Inland	63-66
— Auto	66-67
Reissverschluss	93
Reiten	123
REPARATUREN	96-98
— Auto	126-127
Restaurant	
	44, 54, 71, 105
Rezept	80
Rhabarber	113
Rindfleisch	108
Rom	133
Roman	87
Rüben	115
Rücken	81
Rückwärts fahren	
	126
Ruderboot	123
Rühreier	110
Russland	132
Rutskhen	128
Sahne	109
Salat	113
Salbe	83
Salz	113
Schachtel	77
Schal	92
Schallplatte	91
Schalthebel	129
Scheibenwischer	
	130
Schellfisch	111
Schere	83, 88
Schinken	111
Schirm	35, 72, 93
Schlaftabletten	83
Schlafwagen	29
Schleife	90
Schlittschuhlaufen	
	124
Schloss	69

	Page
Schnupfen	80
Schnürbänder	92
Schokolade	109
Scholle	114
Schottland	130
Schreibpapier	88
Schuhe	57, 92, 96
— putzen	57
— reparieren	96
Schwamm	83
Schweden	132
Schweinebraten	113
Schweiz	133
Schweizerdeutsch	
	12
Schwimmbad	123
See	70
Seekrankheit	45
Segeln	124
SEHENSWÜRDIG-	
KEITEN	67-72
Seide	92
Seife	56, 83
Seilbahn	70
Sellerie	109
Serviette	112
Sherry	114
Sicherheitsnadel	92
Siegellack	88
Skilaufen	124
Socken	92
Soda	114
Sohn	73
Sonne	41
Sonnenbrand	81
— brille	93
— kleid	93
— schutzkreme	84
Spanien	132
Spargel	108
Spät	18, 57
Spaziergang	20
— stock	93
Speck	108
Speisen, bestellen	
	105-107
SPEISEN & TAFEL-	
GERÄT	108-115
Speisekarte	106
Speisewagen	29
Spezialist	82
Spiegel	83, 92, 95
Spinat	114
Spital	82
Spitzenkragen	90
SPORT	121-124
Sportler	121
Spritze	84
Stadt	53, 88
— köfferchen	90
Stecknadel	92
Stiche (Mücken)	81
Strasse	67
Strassenbahn	64, 116
Stecknadeln	93
Strom	70
Strumpfband	91
Strümpfe	92
Stufen	70
Suppe	114
Süssigkeiten	114
Tabak	76
Table d'hôte	105
Tag	66, 125, 137
TAGE DER	
WOCHE	136
Tageslicht	95
Taille	95
Tante	73
Tanz	118
— musik	121
Taschentuch	62, 91
Tasse	110
Taxi	27, 72
Tee	31, 45, 105, 114
Teekanne	114
Telegramm	38, 79
Telephon	25
TELEPHON, AM	25
Teller	107, 112
Tennis	121
Teuer	54, 95
Text	117
Theater	116
— bahn	116
— karten	58, 116
TISCH, AM	105
Tisch	105, 106, 114
Tochter	73
Toilette	22, 55
Tomate	115
Tor (Sport)	122
Turnier	124
Träger	32
TRINKGELD	12
Trüffel	115
Truthahn	115
Tschoslowakei	131
Tür	21, 41, 66
Tüte	48
Uebermorgen	
	72, 138
Ungarn	132
Universität	68
Untergrundbahn	64
Unterhemd	93
Unterhose	92
Unterrock	92
Venedig	133
Verabredung	74
Verband	82
Vergnügungen	
(Ratschläge)	12
Verkehrsampel	128
— polizist	130
— zeichen	128
Verlust, Anmel-	
den	99
Verstopfung	80
Vlissingen	133
Vorgestern	137
Vorhang	41, 57
Vorspeise	113
Vorstellen, sich	73
Wacholder	111
Wagen	64, 125
Wales	130
Wann?	26, 137-138
Warm	41, 71, 86, 119
Warum?	22
Was?	21
Waschen	
	22, 84, 105, 126
Wasser, trinken	
	80, 115, 125
— warm	31, 56

	Page
Wasser, Eis	107
— Mineral	112
Wasser-klosett	22, 55
Wäsche	62-63
Watte	82
Wechselkurs	14, 89
Wecken	56
Wecker	90
Wegweiser	130
Wein	106, 115
Weinkarte	106
Wellen, Haar	85
Wer	57
Whisky	115
Wien	133
Windscheibe	130
Windscheiben-wischer	130
Wo?	22, 42
Woche	137
Wolle	93
Wörterbuch	87

	Page
Wurst	114
ZAHLEN	59, 108
ZAHNARZT, BEIM	103-104
Zahnpasta	84
Zahnschmerzen	81, 103
Zahnstocher	115
ZEIT, MITTEL-EUROPAISCH	10
Zeit, wie spät?	18, 138
— wie lange?	138
— wann?	137
Zeitung	92
— Abend	91
— englisch	37, 55
Zigarren	77
ZIGARRENGE-SCHAFT, IM	76-77
Zigaretten	76
— spitze	77

	Page
Zimmer	52, 56, 58, 105
— mädchen	56-57
— MIETEN	53-55
Zitrone	111
ZOLL	49-51
Zoologischen	68
Zucker	114
Zug (Eisenbahn) allgemeines	10
— Abfahrt	28
— Ankunft	26
— Umsteigen	27, 66
— anhalten	26, 28, 66
— Nacht	61
— wohin?	28, 66
Zugführer	30
Zugluft	41
Zunge	114
Zuschlag	29
Zündhölzer	77
Zündkerze	127, 130
Zwiebel	112

INDEX

The words printed in capitals refer to Sections, in which the subject is dealt with at length.

	Page
Abbreviations, German	144-145
Abroad	79
Accelerator	129
Accident	128
ACCIDENT AND ILLNESS	100-102
ACCOMMODATION	52
Address	20, 63, 75, 103
Admission, to obtain	69
ADVICE, GENERAL	13-14
Aerodrome	46
Aeroplane	46
Africa	131
Ailments, common	80-81, 102
Air	125
Air Mail	78
Air sickness	48
Air Travel	46
Alpenstock	90
Ambulance	100
America	131
American	76
Ammonia	81
AMUSEMENTS, ADVICE ON	12
Ankle	101
Aperient	82
Apologise, to	17
Apple	108
Appointments, making of	74
Apricots	108
ARRIVING BY TRAIN	26-27

	Page
Asia	131
Asparagus	108
Attendant	30, 41
— Female	82
— Male	82
Aunt	73
Australia	131
Austria	13, 14, 131
Back	81, 101
Bacon	108
Bag	33
Ball	122
Band	118
Bandage	82
— (Crepe)	82
BANK, THE	89
Bar	44, 55
Basle	133
Bath	53, 55
Bathroom	55
Battery	129
Beans	108
Bed	53, 102
Beef	108
Beer	108
Belgian	131
Belgium	131
Bell	41
Belt	90
Berlin	133
Berths	30, 44
Bicycle	123
Bill, how to pay	59, 108
Biscuit	109
Bites, mosquito	81
Black pudding	108
Blades, razor	83
Blanket	56

	Page
Blind	41
Blisters	81
Blouse	90
Booking-office (See TRAVELLING BY TRAIN, *Departing*)	30, 65
Book	35, 71, 79, 87
BOOKSHOP AND STATIONER	87-88
Botanical Gardens	68
Bottle	88, 115
— hot-water	56
Bow-tie	90
Box	77
Brakes	127, 129
Brandy	45, 48, 100, 109
Bread	109
Breakfast	31, 105
Breast	107
Bridge	128
Britain, Great	130
Brush, clothes	57, 90
— hair	91
— nail	83
— shaving	83
— tooth	84
Brussels	133
Buffet	34
Building	67
Bus	64, 116
— Hotel	60
— stop	64
Business quarter	53
Butter	105, 109
Cab (*See* Taxi)	

	Page
Cabbage	109
Cabin	43
CAFES, ADVICE ON	9
Cake	109
Calf's head	109
Camera	90
— repairs for	97
Canada	131
Cap, bathing	
	90, 123
Capitals of	
countries	133
Car-ferry	128
Car, motor	125
Carburettor	129
Cards, playing	88
— visiting	73
Carrots	109
Case, attaché	90
— suit	35, 93, 98
Castle	69
Catalogue	71
Cathedral	68
Cauliflower	109
Caviare	109
Celery	109
Chains, wheel	129
CHAMBERMAID,	
THE	56-57
Change, small	
	60, 117
Chauffeur	66
Cheap	54, 95
Cheese	109
CHEMIST	80-84
Chemist	101
Chicken	109
Chocolate	109
Chop	109
Church	67
Cider	109
Cigar	77
Cigarette	76
Cigarette-holder	77
Cinema	118
City	88
Classes (in train)	
	29, 30
Clock, alarm	90
Clothes, brushing	57

	Page
Clothes, mending	63
Clothing, articles	
of (See General	
Shopping	
Vocabulary	90
Clothing, sports	
(See SPORT)	121
Clutch (of motor-	
car)	129
Coat	90
Coffee	105, 109
Cold	41, 107
— chest	80
— head	80, 102
Collars	62, 90
Cologne	30, 133
Colour film	86
Colours	94
Comb	82
Commands, how	
to give	19
COMMON PHRASES,	
English	17-23
German	139-143
Communication	
cord	42
Compartments	
(train)	29
Complaints, of	
charges	60, 108
— of food	107
Constipation	80
Consulate, British	
	23
Corn pads	82
Corns	81
Cost	
34, 35, 44, 46, 47, 95
Cotton	90
Cotton-wool	82
COUNTRIES AND	
NATIONALITIES	
	130-133
Cream	109
— face	82
— sun protection	84
Credit, Letter of	
	49, 89
Cup	110
Currency	10

	Page
Curtains	57
Custard	110
CUSTOMS	49-52
Customs Officer	50
Cut	101, 102
Cutlet	110
Cyclist	123, 129
Czecho-Slovakia	131
Dance-music	121
Dances, names of	
	118
Dance	118
Dark (lighting-	
up)	127
Daughter	73
Day	66, 137
— every	138
Daylight	95
DAYS OF THE	
WEEK	136
Deck	43, 44
— chair	44
Denmark	131
DENTIST, AT	
THE	103-104
Dessert	110
Diarrhoea	80
Dictionary	87
Dinner	
31, 55, 106, 110
Directions, how	
to ask	63-65
Distance, meas-	
urement of	136
District	88
Doctor	82, 100, 101
Door	21, 41, 66
Draught	41
Dress	91
— evening	91
Drink	41, 119
Driving-licence	128
Duck	110
Dutch	50
Duty, Customs	51
Earache	81
Egg, dried	110
Eggs	108, 110

	Page
End	79
ENGAGING	
ROOMS	53-55
Engine, motor	127
England	75, 130
English	18, 63, 66, 76,
	80, 87, 100, 117, 130
English Channel	
	133
En Pension	54
ENTERTAINMENT	
	116
Envelopes	88
Europe	131
Evening	137
— this	62, 98
Exchange, rate of	
	14, 89
EXCURSIONS	63
Expensive	54, 95
Eye-black	82
Family, members	
of	73
Farewells	75
Fault	100
Feet	81
File, nail	83
Film, camera	86, 98
— cinema	117
Fire	55
Fish	110
Flannel	82
Flannels, tennis	93
Flint, lighter	77
Florence	133
Flushing	133
Food, asking	
about	105-106
— ordering	105-107
Football	122
Fork	107, 110
Fortnight	137
France	131
French	50
Friends, inquiring	
for	58
FRIENDS, VISIT-	
ING	73-75
Frontier	26

	Page
Fruit	110
— stewed	114
Funicular	70
Gallon	125, 136
Garage	125, 129
Gargle	82
Garters	91
Gears, of car	
	127, 129
GENERAL ADVICE	13
General Post	
Office	64, 78
Geneva	133
German	18, 74, 87,
	106, 117, 132
GERMAN-ENGLISH	
PHRASES	139-143
Germany	88, 132
Gin	111
Glass	102, 115
Glasses, eye	91, 96
— frame for (*See*	
REPAIRS)	96
— opera	117
— sun	93
Gloves	94
— fur	91
— white	91
Goal	122
Golf	121
Good-afternoon	17
— -bye	18, 75
— -evening	17
— -morning	17
— -night	17, 57
Goods	79
Gowns, evening	91
Gramophone	
records	91
Gravy	111
Greetings, how to	
convey	24, 74
Guard (train)	30
Guide	67, 69, 72
— -book	63
Gums	103
Hair curlers	86
— cut	84

	Page
Hair dryer	86
— net	86
— pins	86
HAIRDRESSER	84-86
Hake	111
Ham	111
Hand	81, 101
Handkerchief	62, 91
Hands, to wash	22
Haste and speed	
	19, 21, 33, 35, 52
Hat	91
Hay-fever	80
Head	80, 101
Headache	81, 102
Head-square	91
Heating	41
Hiring a car	66
Holiday	51
Holland	132
Home, escorting	
	119
Honey	105
Hook of Holland	
	133
Horn, motor	129
Hors d'œuvre	113
Horse-racing	123
Hospital	82
Hot	41, 71, 86, 119
Hotel	52
HOTEL, IN THE	
	55-57
— LEAVING	59-62
— Office	58-59
Hungary	132
Husband	73
Ice	111
Ice-rink	124
ILLNESS AND	
ACCIDENT	100
Influenza	102
INFORMATION,	
LOCAL	11
Interval	117
Inter-zonal	
travel	8
Introductions,	
how to make	73

	Page
Invitations,	
acceptance of	74
Iodine	102
Ireland	130
Italy	132
Jam	111
Journey	26
Kidney	111
Knife	107, 111
Knitting-needles	93
Label	61
Lace-collar	90
Ladies' room	37
Lake	70
Land, to	43, 46, 47
Lamb	111
Late	18, 26, 42
LAUNDRY	62-63
Leather	87
Leek	111
Left	65
Leg	101, 107
Lemon	111
Lens	96
Letters, inquiring	
for	58
— forwarding	61
— of introduc-	
tion	73
— posting	37, 58
LETTER WRITING	24
Lettuce	111
Lift	53
Light	41
— on car	127, 129
Lighter	77
Links, cuff	91
Lint	82
Lip-stick	82, 91
Liqueur	111
Liver	111
Lobster	111
Lock	36, 98
Lorry	128
Loss, reporting	99
Lost Property	
Office	37

	Page
Lounge	56, 106
Luggage (See	
TRAVELLING	
BY TRAIN)	32
— examination	
of	49-52
— handling of	32
— insurance of	33
— left	34
— registration of	32
— van	32, 124
Lunch	111
Magneto	129
Manager	59, 89
Manicure	85
Map	63, 88, 128
Mark, German	
	14, 49
Marmalade	105, 112
Marrow,	
vegetable	115
Massage, face	85
Matches	77
Meal, ordering	
	105, 107
MEALS	11
MEASURES	136
Meat, boiled	108
— cold	110
— roast	108
Medicines (See	
CHEMIST)	80
Melon	112
Memorial	70
Menu	106
MENU	108-115
Messenger	58
Midday	138
Middle	85
Midnight	138
Milan	133
Mile	67
Milk	112
Milk, powdered	110
Minute	57
Mirror	83, 92, 95
MONEY	14
— Austrian	14
— cashing	89

	Page
MONEY	
— changing of	37
— German	14, 49
— Swiss	13
Money-orders	79
Month	138
MONTHS	137
Morning	138
Mosquito-bites	81
Motor-car	125
— coach	46
MOTORING	
	13, 125-130
Mountain	70
Mudguard	129
Munich	133
Museums	67
Mushrooms	112
Music	92
Music	92
Mustard	112
Mutton	112
Nail, finger	85
— file	83
— varnish	83
— varnish-	
remover	83
Name	70, 73, 80
Napkin	112
Naples	133
Nephew	73
Nerve	103
Newspaper	92
— English	37, 55
— evening	91
Niece	73
Night	125
Nightdress	92
No	17, 107
Non-smoker	29, 40
North Sea	133
Norway	132
Novel	87
Number	54, 58, 135
NUMERALS	134-135
Nurse, trained	102
Nursing home	82
OFFICE, HOTEL	
	58-59

	Page
Office. left	
luggage	34
Oil, castor	82
— hair	82, 86
— motor	125, 129
— salad	112
— sunburn	83
Oilsilk	83
Ointment	83
Olives	112
Omelette	112
One-way street	128
Onion	112
Opera	58
Orange	112
Orchestra	117
Overcoat	35, 90
Oysters	112
Pants	92
Paper-bag	48
Paper-clips	88
Parcel	35, 78
Paris	132
Park	68
Parking-place	129
Passport	45, 49
— advice on	9
— examination	
of	45, 49
Paste	88, 112
— tooth	84
Pastry	109
Paying bills	59, 108
Peach	112
Pear	112
Peas	112
Pen	88
Pencils	88
Pepper	112
Petrol	125, 129
— purchase of	125
— rationing (See	
Introduction,	
p. 13)	
— -station	129
— -tank	129
Petticoat	92
PHOTOGRAPHER	
AT THE	86

	Page
Photographs,	
taking	70
Picture	71
-gallery	67, 69
Pie	112
Pillow	31, 56
Pills	83
Pineapple	112
Pins	92
Pipe	77
— -cleaner	77
Place	42
Places (in train)	
	29, 30
Plaster	83
Plate	107, 112
Platform	28, 65
Play (See ENTER-	
TAINMENT)	120
Please	17
Plug, sparking	
	127, 130
Plum	113
Poland	132
POLICE, THE	99
Policeman	100
— -traffic	130
Police-office	23, 99
Pork	113
Porter	32
— night	59
Porthole	44
Postage	78
Postcards	38, 71, 78
Poste restante	79
POST OFFICE	78-80
Potatoes	113
Poultry	113
Pound	136
Powder	83, 92
PRELIMINARIES TO	
TRAVEL	9
Prescription, to	
inquire	80
Print, photo-	
graphic	86
Programme	117
— (radio)	120
PRONUNCIATION	
NOTES ON	15-16

	Page
PRONUNCIATION	
— of Swiss Ger-	
man	12-13
Prunes	113
Public	68
Pullover	92
Pumice-stone	83
Puncture	126
Pyjamas	92
Quality, of goods	95
Questions com-	
mon	19, 22-23
Quinine	83
Rabbit	113
Radiator, of car	125
RADIO	120-121
Radish	113
Ragout	113
Rain	71
Raspberries	113
Rationing	11
Razor	83
— -blade	83
Receipt	60
Refills	88
Refreshment	
buffet	34
Registration of	
foreigners	99
— of letters	78
— of luggage	32
REPAIRS	96-98
Repairs, motor	
	126-127
Reservation of	
seats	29, 46
Restaurant	
	44, 54, 71, 105
— -car	29
Reverse	126, 130
Revue	58
Rhubarb	113
Rice	113
Riding	123
Right	65
River	47, 70
Roll	105, 113

	Page
Rome	133
Room	52, 56, 58
— double	53
— single	53
— sitting	53
ROOMS, ENGAGING	53
— preparation of	55
— vacating	61
Rouge	83, 92
Route	128
ROUTES TO GERMANY	9
Rowing-boat	123
Rug	31, 35, 47, 93
Ruler	88
Russia	132
Safety-pin	92
Sailing	124
Salads	113
Saloon, on ship	44
Salt	113
Salts, bath	82
— fruit	81
Sandwiches	61, 113
Sardines	113
Sauce	114
Saucer	114
Sausage	114
Scarf	92
Scissors	83, 88
Scotland	130
Screen-wiper	130
Sculpture	69
Sealing-wax	88
Sea-sickness	45
Seats (in train)	29
Servants' board	54
Shampoo	84
Sheets	56
Sherry	114
Shirt	62, 91, 92
Shoe	57, 92, 96
Shoe-lace	92
— repairs (See REPAIRS)	96
— cleaning	57
SHOPPING VOCABULARY	90-93

	Page
Short-circuit	127
Shutters	57
Side	85
SIGHT-SEEING	67-72
Sign-post	130
Silk	92
Sizes, in clothes	76, 94
Skating	124
Skid	128
Ski-ing	124
Skirt	92
Sleeping-car	29
Sleeping tablets	83
Sleeves (long, short)	94
Smelling-salts	102
Smoking	118
— compartment	29
Soap	56, 83
— shaving	83
Socks	92
Soda	114
Sole (fish)	114
Son	73
Soup, clear	114
— gravy	114
— pea	112
Souvenir gifts	93
Spain	132
Specialist	82
Speed, maximum	129
Spinach	114
Spoon	107, 114
Sponge	83
SPORT	121-124
Sportsman	121
Spray	83
Stamps	38, 78, 93
Starter, of car	130
Station	26, 28, 61, 65
STATION, AT THE	32
Station, police	37
— tube	64
— -master	37
STATIONER	87-88
Steamer	43
— arrival of	44

	Page
Steamer	43
— departure	43
Steeple-chase	123
Steps	70
Stick, walking	93
Stockings	92
Stomach-ache	81
— -powder	83
Stopping, of tooth	103
Stranger	128
Strawberries	114
Street	67, 128
Studs	93
Sugar	114
Suit, bathing	90, 123
— of clothes	57
Sun	41
— -burn	81
— -dress	93
— glasses	93
— protective cream	84
Supper	114, 118
Supplement (on ticket)	29
Surgeon	82
Suspenders	93
Sweden	132
Sweets	114
Swimming	123
Swiss currency	13
— -German pronunciation	12
SWITZERLAND	12, 133
Syringe	84
Table	105, 106, 114
TABLE, AT	105
Table d'hote	105
Taxi	27, 64, 72
Tea	31, 45, 105, 114
Tea-pot	114
Telegram	38, 79
Telegraph form	79
Telephone	25, 99
TELEPHONING	25
Tennis	121
— racket	121

	Page
Text	117
Thanks, expressing	75, 101
Thank you	17, 72
Theatre, inquiring about	116
THEATRE	116
Things	34, 36
Thread, cotton	91
Throat, sore	102
Ticket, single	30
— return	30
Tickets, booking of	30, 43
— cinema	117
— landing	44
— luggage	33
— platform	30
— theatre	58
Tie	93
— dress	91
Time, asking the	18, 138
TIME, CENTRAL EUROPEAN	10
Time, duration of	138
TIME, PHRASES OF —the clock	138
— — general	137-138
Time, statement of	138
TIME-TABLES	38
TIPPING	12
Tips	60, 67
Toast	105, 114
Tobacco	76
TOBACCONIST, THE	76-77
To-day	71, 137
Together	40
Toilet requisites (See CHEMIST)	80
Tomato	115
To-morrow	72
—, day after	72
Tongue	114
To-night	78

	Page
Tooth, extraction	103
— stopping	103
Toothache	81, 103
Toothpick	115
Tour	69
Tournament	124
Towels	56, 83, 93
— sanitary	83
Town	53
Town hall	68
Towns, common	133
Traffic lights	128
— policeman	130
— signal	128
Trains, advice on	10
— arrival of	26
— changing of	27, 66
— departure of	28
— destination of	28, 66
— night	61
— stopping of	26, 28, 66
Tram	64, 116
Trams, late	116
Travellers' cheques	49, 59, 89
TRAVEL, RUSH HOUR	11
TRAVELLING, ADVICE ON	9-11
— BY AIR	9, 46-49
— BY BOAT	9, 43-45
— BY MOTOR	66-67
— BY TRAIN	26-42
— LOCAL	63-66
Trousers	93
Truffles	115
Trunk	51
Tube, motor	129
Tune	119
Turkey	115
Turnip	115
Tyre, motor	125, 130
Umbrella	35, 72, 93

	Page
Uncle	73
Underground	64
University	68
UTENSILS	108-115
Veal	110, 115
Vegetable	115
Venice	133
Vest	93
Vienna	133
View, good	70
Vinegar	115
VISITING FRIENDS	73-75
Waist	95
Waiter	106
— head	107
Waking up	56
Wales	130
Walk	20
Wash	22, 105, 126
Watch, wrist	93
— repairs to	97
Water, drinking	80, 115, 125
— hot	31, 56
— iced	107
— mineral	112
Way, the	63
WAY, ENQUIRING THE	63-65
Wave, hair	85
— permanent	85
W.C.	22, 55
Week	125, 137
WEEK, DAYS OF	136
WEIGHTS AND MEASURES	136
Welsh	130
What	21
When	26, 137-138
Where	22, 42
Whisky	115
Who	57
Why	22
Wick, lighter	77
Wife	73
Window	21, 40, 48, 55, 106

	Page		Page		Page
Wind-screen	130	Wool	93	Yesterday	137
— wiper	130	Wrist	101	—, day before	137
Wine list	106	Writing paper	88		
Wines	106, 115			Zip-fastener	93
Wing	107	Year	137	Zoological	
WIRELESS	120	Yes	17, 107	gardens	68

6 8 10

Lippe Ilsuan Holzminden S

Gelsenkirchen Dortmund Paderborn Göttingen
Duisburg Hamborn Essen Bochum Warburg Nordhausen
Krefeld-Uerdingen Uggen Korbach Kassel Sonderha
Düsseldorf Wuppertal G E R M
Solingen Cologne Bad Wildungen Mühlhausen Gotha
M'Gladbach Siegen Eisenac
Maastricht Düren Bonn Siegnag Treysa Bebra Ulhersfeld T H U
Liège Aachen Marburg Alsfeld Thürin
Eupen Ahrweiler Neuwied Giessen Fulda W
Verviers Spa Wetzlar Meining
Malmedy Koblenz Ems Schotten Schüchtern
Marche Gerolstein Bad Bad
Daun Homburg Kissingen
Wittlich Kochem Zell Wiesbaden Frankfurt Hanau Schwein
Randen Bingen Offenbach Aschaffenburg Zeil
Libramont Luxemburg Mainz Darmstadt Würzburg
Arlon inburg Trier RHINE-PFALZ Bad Pfung Kitzingen
Saarburg Oberstein Kreuznach stadt Tauberbischofs Neustadt
Thionville Neunkirchen Worms Königshofen Fürth
Verdun Saarlautern SAAR Ludwigshafen Mannheim heim
Gravelotte Metz Saarbrücken Kaiserslautern Speyer Heidelberg Koch Ansbach B
Zweibrücken Landau Sinzheim Leihhorn
Lorraine Bitche Pirmasens WÜRTTEMBERG Hall Ellwangen
Pont-à- Karlsruhe BADEN Aalen Nördlinge
Mousson Sarrebourg Hagenau Pforzheim Rastatt Esslingen Ingo
Nancy Saverne Baden Ludwigsburg Stuttgart
Lunéville Strasbourg Bühl Berneck Blenheim
Meurthe Kehl Horb Tübingen Reutlingen
Epinal St Dié Sélestat Ulm Neu Ulm
Schramberg Hechingen WÜRTTEMBERG Landsbe
48 Colmar BADEN Sigmaringen Biberach
Plombières Freiburg Donau Waldsee Memmin
Vesoul Mülheim schingen Überlingen
Belfort St Weil
Montbéliard Lörrach Blasien Fredrichshafen Kempten
Schaffhausen Konstanz Lake of Li
Doubs Basle Winterthur Constance Bregenz Imm
Besançon Olten Aarau St Dornbirn
Solothurn Zug Gallen Feldkirch Inst
Pontarlier Neuchâtel Aare Luzern Zürich Liechtenstein
L.Neuchâtel Glarus Chur Stadten Lan
Fribourg L.of Schwyz Rhine
Berne Luzern Wild
SWITZERLAND Chia T
St Claude Lausanne Bernese Alps Interlaken Wild.
Montreux St Gotthard Splügen St Moritz Bo
Geneva Jungfrau Chiavenna Adig
L. of Geneva Rhone Brig Locarno Bellinzona I
Simplon 10